D1593061

Holy Dogs and Asses

Holy Dogs and Asses

Animals in the Christian Tradition

LAURA HOBGOOD-OSTER

UNIVERSITY OF ILLINOIS PRESS

Urbana and Chicago

Library of Congress Cataloging-in-Publication Data
Hobgood-Oster, Laura
Holy dogs and asses : animals in the Christian
tradition / Laura Hobgood-Oster.
p.   cm.
Includes bibliographical references and index.
ISBN-13 978-0-252-03213-4 (cloth : alk. paper)
ISBN-10 0-252-03213-6 (cloth : alk. paper)
1. Animals—Religious aspects—Christianity.
I. Title.
BT746.H63   2008
241'.693—dc22   2007016984

To all the dogs of my life:
Beaugart, Cezar, Codi, Bucksnort,
Samson, Sophie, Hooker, Dozier,
Fluffy, Maggie, Stinky, Rumple, Gus,
and many more.

Contents

Preface

> The animal opens before me a depth that attracts me and is familiar
> to me. In a sense, I know this depth: it is my own. It is also that
> which is farthest removed from me, that which deserves the name
> depth, which means precisely *that which is unfathomable to me*.[1]

Georges Bataille, an influential and sometimes controversial twentieth-century French philosopher, opens his *Theory of Religion* with a chapter titled "Animality." Religion, according to Bataille, is the search for a lost intimacy.[2] Other-than-human animals somehow point to this intimacy; thus they have, for most of the history of religions, played a role in the religious life of humans. Paul Waldau, in his introductory essay to *A Communion of Subjects,* poses some of the central questions that those few studying animals and religion or putting forward animal theologies ask: "How have religious traditions and their believers engaged other animals? Have they promoted or prevented obvious harms to the nearby biological individuals outside human communities, or have they ignored them altogether? . . . How have religious traditions handled potential human power over nonhumans?"[3] What do animals have to do with any of it? These questions are being posed with increasing frequency at the beginning of the twenty-first Christian century.

In the year 2000 the Caucus on Animals, Religion, and Ethics gathered officially for the first time at the American Academy of Religion (AAR) annual meeting. There, Carol Adams, author of *The Sexual Politics of Meat,* presented her theory of the absent referent and the role of animals (particularly animals that are eaten by humans) in contemporary Western culture. In 2002 this new academic caucus applied for status as a formal consultation with the AAR. The group's application was rejected based, in part, on the sense that the study of animals and religion overlapped too much with the study of religion and ecology and, to the amazement of feminists, with the study of women and religion. But in 2003 the Consultation on Animals and Religion received formal recognition and thus a three-year trial period (this trial period was renewed for a second three-year consultation status through 2008). Along with Paul Waldau, I have cochaired the group over this period.

Is there a resurgence in the study of animals as an integral part of human religious life and history? Is there a recognition that animals have always formed a central component of religion but for complex reasons have been excluded from its formal analysis? Whatever the impetus, other-than-human animals are entering the conversation as a subject of religious study and theological reflection. Courses on animals and religion appear in course listings at various colleges and universities, scholarly conferences devoted to this particular area of study convene with increasing regularity, and the AAR consultation receives dozens of presentation proposals for the annual meetings each year. It is, at the very least, a growing field of inquiry and one that is increasingly interdisciplinary. As Marc Bekoff, a professor of biology, stated in a recent article, "Animals are 'In.'"[4]

But why are animals becoming a progressively interesting subject in the history of religions and, in the case of this book, in the history of Christianity? And what might it mean to return animals to the sanctuary? My contention is that animals have never left the sanctuary, they have just been forgotten or ignored. As the philosophers of the Enlightenment elevated humanism, as modern animal-free technologies replaced animal-based technologies (automobiles, for example, replacing horses in the everyday lives of people, or tractors instead of oxen on farms), and as myriad other cultural shifts removed animals from the daily lives of many increasingly urbanized Western Christians, the few animals left in the lives of most European and North American Christians were either domesticated pets (a recent category) or were already dead and being served as a meal. Real animals disappeared from life and from ideas of history as well as practical theology and liturgy.

But humans are animals. And as questions continue to emerge about the human relationship to animals, they also enter the field of religious studies. Thus at the beginning of the twenty-first century, animals and religion became a more broadly recognized discussion in the academic study of religion. They not only are included in the historical and comparative fields but also are becoming the subjects of constructive theological reflection.

I contend, and hopefully this work shows, that without animals a complete history of Christianity or of any religious tradition, or of humanity as a whole, is impossible. Animals have always been present with us in some form or another. And the intimacy that Bataille posits as the goal of religion is lacking if animals are excluded. Therefore, in the hope of adding to the work of Waldau, McDaniel, Linzey, Bekoff, McFague, Adams, and many others, I delve into some animals in the history of the Christian tradition.

Acknowledgments

Although this book is dedicated to the many dogs in my life, there are a number of humans without whom the work would not have been possible.

First, I want to thank the community of Southwestern University—particularly the faculty and students in the Department of Religion and Philosophy. Also, thank you to the administration for providing me a sabbatical during which I completed the bulk of this research and writing. Southwestern University fosters a space of creativity and freedom, and such a space allows for a study such as this one to take place.

Second, there are images throughout the text, both pictured and referenced. To the ones who created these and the ones who preserve them, your devotion to these irreplaceable works of art is appreciated by generation after generation. I ask readers to look at the list of images and, if you are ever in the presence of one of the originals, please thank those who continue to oversee their preservation.

It is important to acknowledge Liz Dulany, my editor at University of Illinois Press, and Cope Cumpston, art director for the Press. Both gave me much needed feedback and assistance in the process. Without an editor's support, a book would remain hidden.

While I will certainly miss mentioning some names, here are just a few who helped along the way: Belden Lane, Paul Waldau, Jan Symons, Jay McDaniel, Richard Valantasis, Maria Johnson, and Waylon Christopher. Thank you all for your encouragement and input.

Finally, and with my most heartfelt appreciation, I acknowledge my family. The ideas in this book developed over years and in the midst of a group of people who love animals and taught me that there are many species in a community and many ways to think about Christianity—my parents (Chris and Cary Meade), my siblings (Cary Lou, Benjamin, Stephanie), and my husband, Jack. He listened to so many ideas, helping me sort through them over dinner and on long walks. Without his patient ear, my ramblings would never have come to fruition.

Holy Dogs and Asses

1. Weaving and Roaring

*Animals and a Religious Studies–Centered
Methodological Bricolage*

Animals first entered the imagination as messengers and promises.[1]

Loreto Aprutino sits on the hills overlooking the Abruzzo countryside in an area of Italy rarely visited by tourists. Each spring, on the Monday following Pentecost, the town celebrates its patron saint, San Zopito.[2] The saint's relics sit in an altar on the side of the main church (San Pietro Apostolo), at the top of a winding road, and, as always, not too far from the town's old fortress. But on the day of the town's celebration, San Zopito's relics leave the safety of the altar and travel through the town as part of a major procession. In the midst of the festival attention quickly diverts from the gold-encased remains of this early martyr to a large white ox as it moves through the village in a stately march. *Il Bui de San Zopito,* the Ox of Saint Zopito, marks every aspect of San Zopito's commemoration and brings living animals to the heart of Christian ritual and story.

As the legend goes, the Catholic Church transported the relics of the saint from the catacombs of San Callixtus in Rome to Loreto Aprutino in order to provide the people with the efficacious treasure. While farmers toiled in the fields outside the town, the procession passed by, apparently either unnoticed or ignored by the farm workers. But il Bui recognized the power of the relics and, still attached to his plow, halted, then knelt in reverence. The lesson told over and over again in Christian story: animals often understand and acknowledge the sacred in their midst when humans fail to comprehend.[3]

For almost three hundred years this scene, with some fascinating embellishment, has come alive again on the streets of Loreto Aprutino. The ox, called a *simbolo insostituibile dell'intera comunita religiosa* (an irreplaceable symbol of the religious community), wears a carefully prepared headdress of bells and colorful ribbons (red, green, white, and yellow). Draped in a scarlet red cloak with images of various saints attached, he becomes a *tramite* (a way through or a vehicle) of the divine, an *elemento soprannaturale*.[4] Interestingly, one of the saint's images, carefully taped onto the red scarlet cloak, appears to be Saint Anthony Abbot, the earliest saint associated with blessings of animals.

Il Bui carries a young girl dressed in white and trimmed in gold. She holds a red carnation in her mouth and a white umbrella over her head. An entirely other area of representation comes through here as she incarnates the angel sent by the saint. Il Bui stops at various points throughout the city, but the major event takes place at the town square (the piazza). Throughout the day the piazza prepares for his arrival with local marching bands and booths covered with food or offering games. Suddenly people begin to gather, more people than one imagines could possibly live in or near this small town. The square fills as row upon row of ritual participants and observers await il Bui's arrival, along with the arrival of the relics (though the ox seems much more fascinating to the crowds). Disabled participants move to the front of the crowd in order to be closer to the power of the relics and, maybe, to the supernatural representative, the ox.

Il Bui comes slowly down the road, a lumbering yet graceful figure, and reaches the center of the piazza. There he turns around, led carefully by his handlers, and prepares for the relics to pass. Year after year participants wit-

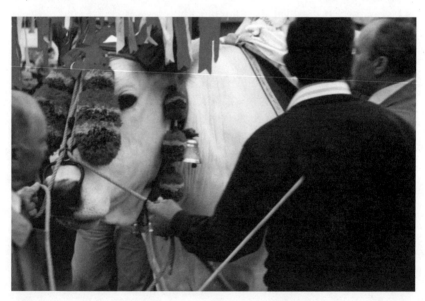

Il Bui de San Zopito festival. Photo taken by author, May 2002.

Il Bui de San Zopito festival. Photo taken by author, May 2002.

ness the miracle as the saint's relics move by and the huge ox kneels to the ground in reverence.

But the celebration is not complete yet. An air of solemnity and respect replaces the festive cheers as the procession continues up the hill to the church with the ox following. Lines of children dressed in white, bearers of various religious artifacts and symbols, and groups of the devout chant religious incantations, including, "Praise to holy Mary, mother of the cattle." For centuries the ox followed the relics into the sanctuary, knelt before the altar, and created a pile of manure (indeed, he defecated in the church)—a sign of a good harvest to come. However, according to the residents of the town, the church decided to stop that practice in the mid-twentieth century and townspeople with cloths prepare to catch any excrement that might fall while the ox is in the sanctuary. Still, when manure emerges from the momentarily sacred animal along the procession route, it is seen as a good sign for the summer crops. Maybe fertility rites subsided a bit as agriculture became less central to the everyday lives of individuals in the community, or maybe ox manure in the church was not looked upon fondly by the ecclesiastical hierarchy. Possibilities abound for change in this final ox-centered enactment of the feast.

Needless to say, this animal-rich ritual begs for interpretation and participation. From the final act of depositing a pile of manure in the sanctuary to the initial spectacular preparation of the ox, researchers certainly imagine various pre-Christian, nature-based ("pagan") influences on the celebration. But such interpretation is not the primary purpose of this study. Rather, the question of what is going on with the ox, who is, arguably, the central actor in this festival, underlies the research. How is an animal symbol and subject, alive and involved, a vehicle of the divine and a faithful example to all witnesses? When do and did other-than-human animals enter and leave the stage of Christianity and what does that mean?[5]

Animals have functioned on the periphery, if even located at that marginal point, in the history of Christian practice and theology. But they are not absent from the scene altogether. As a matter of fact, they are present in myriad practices, texts, and stories. Examining this presence is the core of my research. The trajectories of the impact of animal presence direct the project. Although it is significant to recognize animals in Christianity in order to fully understand this aspect of human culture, it is also requisite to acknowledge the impact of Christianity on animals. In other words, Christian theology and practices impact animals in dramatic ways, even though animals seem to have no input whatsoever with respect to theology and these practices (then again, very few humans had input into the official theological constructs for the first two thousand years of the tradition).

Is Christianity, as Andrew Linzey poignantly asks, "irredeemably speciesist," and if so, what does that really mean, not just for Christians but for every other species that inhabits the earth with humans?[6] Or is it, as Peter Singer states, "beyond dispute that mainstream Christianity, for its first 1800 years, put non-human animals outside its sphere of concern"?[7] With these questions in mind, I look at the wide variety of animals in the history of Christianity through a different lens—a lens that, first and foremost, simply acknowledges their presence. While this work does not attempt to look at all animals or to cover all periods in Christian history, it suggests that a different gaze finds animals in the pictures and offers examples of those alternative images for consideration.

Still, one might ask, why look at animals within the history of the Christian tradition at all?[8] I return to this question in the final pages of the study and throughout, in subtle ways at times. The question "Why look?" comes from both the experience of the author and from the myriad methods and theories explained below. In short, Christianity seems to embody the pinnacle of the religion of "the human" or, more accurately, of "man." The divine (male god) incarnates in a human-divine (male person). Indeed, there is justice-oriented potential manifest in this embodiment or enfleshed aspect of Christianity, but that potential is outweighed by the patriarchal systems that, from early in its history, mark the rest of the story and personality of this religious tradition. I expand on that topic later, but suffice it to say that Christianity's tendencies to focus on the male human and his individual salvation has, historically, placed the tradition within easy grasp of domination systems of all types. Such systems must always be challenged. In the early years of the twenty-first Christian century (as Western centuries are counted under the assumption of Christian authority over calendars), census figures indicate that one-third of the world's human population, roughly two billion of the six billion people on the planet, claim Christianity as their religion. It is the largest recognized religious system in history.[9]

Yet various sources tell a different story, reveal a different image, of animals in the history of this overtly male dominant, humanocentric religious tradition. Artwork, hagiography, oral traditions (later recorded in written form), and important legends reveal a close connection in Christian thought between humans and the natural world. Stories and images of animals abound. I contend that these animals are not always or only symbolic or metaphoric but are often subjects, actors of these sacred dramas in a more complete sense. Images and narratives contain multiple encodings and decodings. Often the animals presented in words and images are sacred; they exhibit agency and play an active role in the unveiling of the holy.

From an ecological and justice-oriented perspective, we must also look at animals because they represent one of the major binaries in human culture and domination consciousness that must be broken down. As long as humans understand ourselves to be totally other than animals, all domination systems will continue. Again, this idea will be fleshed out below, but feminist theories considerably shape the context of my response to "Why look?"

Additionally, we must look at animals because if we do not, an entire aspect of human history is lost. Can we really comprehend that which is "human" without comprehending the close "other"—the animal? This term— "animal"—addressed immediately below, is problematic in and of itself. But humans have not lived isolated in a bubble away from other animal species. A central principle of environmental history recognizes that humans cannot be understood apart from the ecologies that, at least in part, shape us. Therefore, to engage in a history of the Christian tradition without considering the other-than-human animals that are part of this history is to deal with parts, not wholes. It results in a partial history, one that is incomplete and, in the long run, invalid. A complete history of the Christian tradition necessarily includes all of the animals that are part of it. Again, this work does not claim to be such a complete history; the work of retelling the story of animals in the history of Christianity needs to be shared by many voices.

Rather, it points to examples that recognize holes in the story, holes that are filled at least in part by the inclusion of animals.

Finally, why do I choose to use the term "animal"? One could easily argue that my use of this designation for an other-than-human species, when indeed we humans are animals also, simply reinforces the binary of human/animal. This same question comes through in myriad discussions of animals and humans. Answers vary. I choose to use "animal" to refer to the many other-than-human species emerging throughout the Christian story—spiders, dogs, lions, ravens, otters, asses—because throughout its history Christianity itself separates humans from nonhuman animals in dramatic fashion. Indeed, it should be acknowledged from the outset that Christianity generates a gulf between human animals and all other animals that might be impossible to bridge. Without outlining all of those complex claims, suffice it to say that orthodox Christianity claims humans (and not all humans at that) as the focus of God's plan for salvation. God incarnates the one and only time in a male human. So in many potent ways Christianity reinforces the binary signification of human/animal, just as it, through the same incarnation, re-inforces the binaries of male/female, black/white, and heaven/earth, to name just a few. This historical fact cannot be denied. Whether certain groups of Christians only ordain males because Christ is a male or only accept humans as the subjects of salvation because Christ is a human or force black people out of worship because they are not white and therefore not considered fully human, Christianity is, in many of its historical forms, anthropocentric, sex-ist, racist, and—some, including myself, add this to the list—speciesist. Thus to be honest to the history of this tradition, it makes sense to use the term "animal" with all of its inclusive/exclusive and oppressive connotations.

Indeed, by using the word "animal" I choose to emphasize how prob-lematic it is. What do we mean by "animal" as opposed to "human"? The taken-for-grantedness of this division must be questioned but rarely is. I hope to make the binary seem absurd, the utter distinction seem outlandish. A baptized lion, a preaching dog, and a chorus of birds praising the Creator all bring into question the actuality of separating the human animal from all other animals. It certainly raises the question of whether this distinction is divinely ordained or whether it is, undoubtedly, an ultimate privilege created for and by humans. Simultaneously, the orthodoxy of "male human being as the only divine incarnate" reinforces every possible binary. Therefore the problems embedded in "human" and "animal" as distinct terms and catego-ries must constantly lurk beneath the surface of the text and, on occasion, explode out of the text.

Still, the designation "animal" carries intense, complicated weight that must remain integral to this analysis. In his lecture "The Animal that Therefore I Am (More to Follow)" Jacques Derrida points out the difficulties of the word:

> Yes, *animal,* what a word!
>
> *Animal* is a word that men have given themselves the right to give. These humans are found giving it to themselves, this word, but as if they had received it as an inheritance. They have given themselves the word in order to corral a large number of living beings within a single concept: "the Animal," they say. And they have given themselves this word, at the same time according themselves, reserving for them, for humans, the right to the word, the name, the verb, the attribute, to a language of words, in short to the very thing that the others in question would be deprived of, those that are corralled within the grand territory of the beasts: the Animal. . . . Men would be first and foremost those living creatures who have given themselves the word that enables them to speak of the animal with a single voice and to designate it as the single being that remains without a response, without a word with which to respond.[10]

So throughout this book the word "animal" designates those beings distinguished by "man" as other than, but in so doing recognizes this artificial, dominating, abusive, and absurd distinction. The stories and images within both reinforce and subvert the distinction, questioning use of the word.

Methods

In her seminal study of gender and representation, *Carnal Knowing: Female Nakedness and Religious Meaning in the Christian West,* Margaret Miles suggests that in Christian history "an understanding of oneself as body was produced by gendered religious practices and recorded in texts and visual images that represented men's and women's bodies as symbolic of different religious meanings."[11] She continues by explaining that representations act certain ways in society, that they simultaneously "reflect social practices and attitudes" but also "re-present, reinforce, perpetuate, produce, and reproduce them."[12] After tracing representations of naked and nude (predominantly female) bodies throughout the history of Christianity and drawing fascinating conclusions regarding the impact of such representations on gendered roles in the Christian West, Miles, referencing Foucault, challenges the "essentialist project" of some feminist studies and forwards the advantage of balancing a "productivity hypothesis" with a "repressive hypothesis."[13] In short, her examination of representation suggests that gender formation is both coercive and educative, that human society controls by repressive power and productive socialization. Humans are gendered through a variety of cultural practices and imposed or selected norms.[14]

But what happens to the subjects or objects of a variety of representational strategies when those subjects or objects are animals but not human animals? How does the system work when the living beings who are real or symbolic function in a different system that does not (and many would claim cannot) read the representations as humans are assumed to do? In other words, when animals are represented by (male) humans to (male) humans but the primary impact of objectification falls upon the animals themselves, what does that mean for the animals, if indeed it means anything at all? Certainly it means something for them, even if it does not mean something to them because they are not active participants in the same signification system. When humans represent animals and, therefore, tell ourselves what and who they (the animals) are in relationship to us, animal subjectivity or objectivity and human subjectivity form simultaneously. We humans understand ourselves differently because of the way animals are used as symbols, and humans understand animals differently. But what of the real animals? Because of the assumed and often enacted power of humans over animals, such representation impacts animals as much as humans, though in different ways.

The purpose of this study is to examine a variety of representations of animals in the stories of Christianity. Representations in hagiographies, visual art in religious worship settings, sacred texts, and, finally, in lived rituals provide the foundational material. Although this study spans the entire two-thousand-year history of Christianity, it does not attempt to cover everything in that history. Such a task would be enormous. Increasingly, scholarship that includes animals in Christian history is emerging, and there is no reason to be redundant in this examination. This book also offers the possibility of focus on particular animals; one chapter, therefore, looks exclusively at just one other species—the dog.

The thesis I offer is based on recovering an understanding of the relationship between humans and animals within the history of Christian traditions. Do certain patterns suggest cultural continuities and shared symbols? Are animals legitimized or denigrated in the sacred history of this multifaceted religious tradition? What developments are linked to changes in these representations and experiences of human and animal? What transformations take place in these relationships and how do these transformations point toward other historical patterns? In order to explore these questions, feminist theories and methods are integral, as is a willingness to break out of traditional epistemological categories, as feminist theorists so often do.

As should be the case with such a study, serious and complex methodological questions must be raised from the beginning. How does one study the manifestations of a particular aspect of a religious system both broadly and with particularity? What methods come into play? Traditional methods are incapable of addressing the complexity of this study, at least in isolation from one another. Therefore, a combination of approaches is requisite: the study of popular religion/folk culture, an examination of textual traditions (for example, recorded hagiographical texts), investigation into ritual and performance, and feminist analysis, most specifically, ecofeminist analysis. The encounter of historical theology, feminist theories, historical anthropology, art history, and contemporary ethnographic studies marks this attempt.

To a certain extent I follow the pattern of Jean-Claude Schmitt, who, in his book *The Holy Greyhound: Guinefort, Healer of Children since the Thirteenth Century,* which focuses on medieval history, states that "new concerns and new approaches require a new methodology. . . . Traditional medieval history is for the most part unaware of the oral tradition, literary history is too concerned with a narrative's formal and aesthetic characteristics, religious history is too inclined to view 'popular religion' as a dim, deviant and irrational reflection of the religion of elites, while folklorists all too often lack a historical perspective. . . . The ethnology of 'complex societies' and the anthropology of 'preliterate' societies offer the historian not merely information but new methods."[15] The same is true for the entire study of animals and Christianity. For example, the history of visual arts is central to this discussion, but my concerns are not primarily aligned with those of traditional art historians. Rather, this study examines the role of the visual arts in situ (in the place for which they were created), in other words, what can be gleaned from these images in worship settings, in churches. So in "The Granted Image" I ponder "dogs" (*Canis familiaris*) specifically. What are so many dogs doing in artwork in churches? They appear peaking out from underneath the table or standing firmly at the side of saints. Dogs playfully engage the main characters in a sculpture or sleep quietly at the foot of Jesus. Of course, they also represent heretics or the hounds of hell. What happens when dogs are almost omnipresent in the visual setting of religious ritual? Are they symbol, are they real, or are they both simultaneously?

Another example involves contemporary ritual studies, but my approach is not purely from early-twenty-first century cultural studies or religious anthropology. So the question is, How do animals function at a blessing of the pets/animals? Of course, ideas of religion and culture laid out by Clifford Geertz (along with the myriad critiques of his suggestions), along with Victor Turner's performance and ritual theory, undergird many of the ideas presented in the study of this ritual. I examine the increasing popularity of blessings of the animals/pets in pockets of late-twentieth- and early-twenty-first-century U.S. society and raise questions about its meaning. Some churches use it as an evangelism tool to bring in young families, hardly focusing on the animals themselves. Other churches incorporate words and actions that suggest animals are or can be a real part of the Christian community. This anthropological approach to ritual study requires a methodology distinct from that necessary for probing into a thirteenth-century textual and oral tradition telling the life of a saint, for example. But both research settings are requisite to understanding the role of animals in the history, and the present, of Christianity.

In addition to theories concerning representation and contemporary ritual studies, feminist and ecofeminist methods underlie the entire project, particularly as ecofeminism enters the realm of environmental history and the history of religions. As stated eloquently by Carol Adams:

> What remains for all of us is a task of personal and mythic archaeology, the reinspection of old terrain. We ourselves are buried under layers of categories that construct species difference as a meaningful ethical determinant. We can no longer allow the bishop and other patriarchal knowers to determine our knowledge. Those issues identified by feminist theology as central to patriarchal religion—issues such as the subordination of experience to authority, the rigid conceptualization of "God" as Father and monarch, the notion of the separate, atomistic self—are also central to the idea that animals can be objects or instruments, and that our relationship with the divine trumps their inviolability.[16]

So the ecofeminist theories of Adams, nature/culture theories of philosopher of science Donna Haraway, nuanced gaze theories from Laura Mulvey and John Berger, feminist theories of representation of Margaret Miles (as mentioned above), constructs of animals and representation developed by Steve Baker and Jacques Derrida, and epistemological frameworks constructed by Michel Foucault are among the theories and methods that combine to inform my multipronged approach.

First and foremost, this is an ecofeminist project. Ecofeminism claims that all dualisms and binary oppositional forms must be dismantled in order for oppressive systems in their entirety to end; otherwise, oppressive systems continue to dominate. Thus male/female, spirit/matter, and human/animal function together to reinforce systematic oppression—the spiritual male human dominates the embodied (matter-ed) female animal.[17] These binaries extend to heaven/earth, white/nonwhite, culture/nature, and so on. Therefore I contend that the project of rethinking animals in religious histories (and Christianity in this case) connects directly to the ecofeminist focus on dismantling all oppressions because as long as one binary still maintains normative status, all binaries can potentially reestablish even if momentarily silenced.

Feminist gaze theory, particularly that suggested by Laura Mulvey and Teresa de Lauretis, informs the project, though with the caveat that their theories address cinema specifically and neither includes ideas about the subject-object status of humans-animals; rather, both focus on theories of gender. But this is an ecofeminist project and their feminist theories concerning representation and control are provocative for my research as well. Central to Mulvey's thesis is the idea that "cinematic codes create a gaze, a world, and an object, thereby producing an illusion cut to the measure of desire." Dominant cinema highlights a "woman's to-be-looked-at-ness," thus determining the representation of "woman." The gaze through the camera and at the screen is the dominant male gaze with female as subject.[18] In *Alice Doesn't: Feminism, Semiotics, Cinema*, de Lauretis continues this look into language and representation, connecting it to a feminist critique of structuralism:

> They used it to illustrate the concept of system, Saussure's *langue* and Levi-Strauss's structure, systems of rules that cannot but be obeyed if one is to communicate, speak, or participate in the social symbolic exchange; and precisely for this reason their theories have been considered pernicious or at least of little value to those eager to dismantle all systems of power. . . . "Whoever defines the code or the context, has control . . . and all answers which accept that context abdicate the possibility of redefining it." The point seems to be, one must be willing to "begin an argument," and so formulate questions that will redefine the context, displace the terms of the metaphors, and make up new ones.[19]

These theories lead me to ask similar questions about animals and representation. Who has the power of the gaze? What does this power of representation do to animals? Can the context be redefined, the metaphors displaced, and new ones made up? And on a more basic level, can the simple fact of pointing out the representations, analyzing them, thinking them, lead to subversion and resistance?

In his essay "Sending: On Representation," Jacques Derrida outlines the myriad transformations in representation throughout Western history. Since this study of animals in Christian history examines different periods of history, keeping in mind the shifts in "representation" as suggested by Derrida proves helpful. He posits that, if we follow Heidegger, "the Greek world did not have a relation to what-is as to a conceived image or a representation (here *Bild*). There what-is is presence; and this did not, at first, derive from the fact that man would look at what-is and have what we call a representation (*Vorstellung*) of it as the mode of perception of a subject." In the Middle Ages, to "'be something that is' means to belong to the created order; this thus corresponds to God according to the analogy of what-is." In other words, "what-is" relates as "en creatum."[20]

Derrida then shifts to the modern period, when, according to Heidegger, what-is "consists in an object (*Gegenstand*) brought before man, fixed, stopped, available for the human subject who would possess a representation of it." So in the Cartesian or post-Cartesian period, "what-is is determined as an object present *before* and *for* a subject in the form of *repraesentatio*."[21] As this study moves through various periods and searches for representations of animals in Christian history, these differing perceptions of the state of representation loom large. So as Hegel "reminds us regularly of the limits of representation insofar as it is unilateral, only on the side of the subject," we must also take into account that representation has not always been understood as generating from the human (male) subject only, but from the represented or from the divine. In other words, reading all animals as only and always symbolic or as only and always referenced back to the human subject is a modern and postmodern move. Unless we examine earlier texts in different representational contexts, we will fail to comprehend all the potential meanings of these texts.

Additional questions of representation, subject and object, ponder humans as a different order within the whole. Foucault addresses this topic in his classic work *The Order of Things*. Here he suggests that it is a "profound relief" to realize that "man is only a recent invention, a figure not yet two centuries old, a new wrinkle in our knowledge, and that he will disappear again as soon as that knowledge has discovered a new form."[22] But at this point Foucault proceeds to analyze an image, *Las Meninas* by Velasquez (1646). His analysis speaks volumes to ideas of representation that I address throughout the study. Without going into extreme detail, there is a dog in the painting. Whereas Foucault interprets each and every human figure, from the painter representing himself gazing from behind his own canvas to the mirror that reflects the king and queen he paints to the princess and other human onlookers, in detail, he has this to say regarding the dog in the context of the scene:

> The entire picture is looking out at a scene for which it is itself a scene. A condition of pure reciprocity manifested by the observing and observed mirror, the two stages of which are uncoupled at the lower corners of the picture: on the left canvas with its back to us, by means of which the exterior point is made into pure spectacle; to the right the dog lying on the floor, the only element in the picture that is neither looking at anything nor moving, because it is not intended, with its deep reliefs and the light playing on its silky hair, to be anything but an object to be seen.[23]

A fascinating shift occurs in Foucault's analysis of representation here. Though "man" is a recent invention, "animals" must still be the consummate other and always remain object. I would argue against Foucault's interpretation of the image and offer instead the possibility that the observed and the observers in this image include the dog, who just happens to be taking a nap, and that the image would be incomplete with the "animal."

In this section on methodology, the groundwork for the major methods employed throughout the study is established. At times, in each individual chapter, I explain my methods more directly and in more detail.

Is It Symbolic or Is She Real?

> Fragment 14: But mortals believe that the gods are born,
>   having clothes and speech and bodies like their own.
> Fragment 15: But if cattle (or horses) or lions had hands,
>   and were able to draw with their hands and do works as humans do,
>   horses would draw the forms of gods like horses,
>   and cows like cows, and figure their bodies
>   the same as they themselves have. (Xenophanes)[24]

In the sixth century BCE, Xenophanes raised the question of anthropomorphism and the divine. He suggested that the polytheism marking Greek religious life was a mere projection of humans into the divine realm. God is in human form because humans are the ones creating the representation. Such an argument is easily extended into human representations of animals.

As Steve Baker states eloquently in his book *Picturing the Beast*, "The problem is not only to modify the ways in which animals may be represented pictorially or rhetorically in the culture. It is just as important to open up ways of thinking about animals which are currently discouraged or closed off, and to work out whose interests are served by their present closure. A prime example is the denial of the animal . . . by proposing that stories must be properly understood not to be about animals but about something else entirely."[25] Distinct cultural patterns and symbol systems shape human experiences of and relationship to other living beings in our environments. Patterns are encoded in visual representations (a pig is presented as a strip of bacon), in language (animals are referred to as "it" rather than as "he" or "she"),[26] and in daily, pragmatic ritual performances (a homeless animal is often "put to sleep" and treated as a nuisance).[27] The societies that have formed around, influenced, and been influenced by Christianity in its European and North American settings and manifestations have informed many of these cultural patterns and symbol systems in profound ways. Animals are regarded as subordinate, irrational, and soul-less beings whose primary purpose is based on a theory of utilitarianism that places human beings at the top of a hierarchy. Animals exist for human consumption, labor, and aesthetic or emotional pleasure alone. Intrinsic value and direct relationship between animals and the sacred is denied.[28]

But has this cultural pattern been static, or has some transformation of understanding occurred? Did animals once engage humans and God, within Christianity, differently, at least in some stories or images? If so, why would it matter or what could it affect? How did and does Christianity shape the role of animals as solely utilitarian, and divinely ordained to be so, and how did or does Christianity challenge this premise?

John Berger suggests that "[i]f the first metaphor was animal, it was because the essential relation between man and animal was metaphoric."[29] So, he continues, animals are seen "in eight out of the twelve signs of the zodiac" and as "the sign of each of the twelve hours of the day" for Greeks. But something distinguished "man" from animals, "the human capacity for symbolic thought, the capacity which was inseparable from the development of language in which words were not mere signals, but signifiers of something other than themselves. Yet the first symbols were animals."[30]

Carol Adams adds the concept of the "absent referent" to the discussion of animals and representation, and specifically meat eating:

> The animals have become absent referents, whose fate is transmuted into a metaphor for someone else's existence or fate. Metaphorically, the absent referent can be anything whose original meaning is undercut as it is absorbed into a different hierarchy of meaning; in this case the original meaning of animals' fates is absorbed into a human-centered hierarchy. . . . The absent referent is both there and not there. It is there through inference, but its meaningfulness reflects only upon what it refers to because the originating, literal, experience that contributes the meaning is not there. We fail to accord this absent referent its own existence.[31]

Adams connects sexual violence, racism, and meat eating, interconnecting these cultural domination systems, which she designates as "intertwined oppressions." Animal—and woman and notwhite—all become absent in reality, as literal, but are subsumed under hierarchy-preserving representation. Thus a dead cow is a hamburger or a filet, not a dead cow whose flesh is being eaten.

Certainly the same general concept of the absent referent is true in animal representation in many of the varied texts—visual, written, oral, ritual—that provide the basis for this study. The "literal" animal is absent, replaced by the metaphorical or symbolic animal. In and of itself that statement is fairly obvious, maybe too obvious. However, if one reads all of these texts with a radical, subversive eye of resistance, the real animal might emerge again. So what is the context for animals, sometimes even animal saints? It could be argued that most of the examples I present here are stories of animals that are purely symbolic, that "real" animals are never present, that a version of the absent referent rules. However, when one attends to the roles of the actors, particularly the active roles of the animals in these stories, the roles might reverse. Through their agency might animals subvert the "power" and "control" of the humans and elevate the status and piety of the animal? Who is subject, who is object, and who is actor in these stories and images? That is sometimes left to the interpretation of the hearer of the story, seer of the image, or witness to the event.

Central to my thesis is the idea that reading animals as only and always symbol is escapist and serves to reinforce human superiority and dominance. Animals, as real in history and in body, can be denied reality as fully living beings because they can be relegated to the powerful but disempowering category of symbol. The reality of animals and the animal must be restored and the gaze returned. It is also a trap of modernity and postmodernity to always assume that animals in art, legend, story, and ritual could only be symbolic. Richard Bauckham, in his essay "Jesus and the Wild Animals," suggests that academic studies of New Testament period literature fail in their approach to animals: "References to nature in the NT, especially the Gospels, have been persistently understood from the perspective of modern urban people, themselves wholly alienated from nature, for whom literary references to nature can only be symbols or picturesque illustrations of a human world unrelated to nature. But once the prevalent modern ideology is questioned, as it must be today, we are freed to read the NT differently. We can recognize that, in continuity with the OT tradition, it assumes that humans live in mutuality with the rest of God's creation, that salvation history and eschatology do not lift humans out of nature."[32] Although it might be tempting to look at all animals in human stories that embed meaning (sacred texts) as symbolic, I suggest that doing so is part of the process that minimizes the significance of real animals while elevating humans above all other animals. Therefore, throughout the study, recognition of animals as symbol is part of the analysis, but recognition of animals as "real" is also integral. Rereading the texts in the context of cultures for whom animals are real, constantly present in various roles, is requisite.

Sources and Audience

The official texts of orthodox Christianity present various images of animals in the tradition. In his commentary on *Genesis,* for example, Augustine states, "Here we should note how all of the animals are grouped together and yet kept separate. Scripture says that man was made on the same day as the beasts; for they are all alike earthly animals. Yet on account of the excellence of reason, according to which man is made to the image and likeness of God, it speaks of him separately, after it had finished speaking of the other earthly animals."[33] Although such formal theological texts are integral to the study of animals and Christianity, for the purposes of this study, popular religion or folk culture is also relevant. Certainly the central texts of orthodox, literate Christianity are included, particularly in the chapters that deal with historical contexts and shifting mental frameworks. In other cases, when these central texts are not included, the reader will be directed to other sources because the primary concern is popular Christianity as well as more formal or official theological constructions.

That statement alone proves problematic. The working definition of "popular religion" for this study is most clearly explained with two examples. First, throughout medieval Europe legends of saints were told in various forms. The lives of saints—hagiographies—provided examples to the masses of how they should live; images of these lives still adorn the walls of churches throughout Europe. People learned the stories by hearing them repeatedly and by seeing the images. Therefore, both the hagiographical accounts, as recorded by the literate classes, and the visual images, in situ, provide "texts" for this study. Rather than art commissioned by elites for galleries or private homes, art positioned in churches is the focus. Rather than texts written for theological elites, hagiographical accounts of the lives of saints provide the textual stories.

A second example of popular religion as approached by this study involves contemporary ritual. Although a very small (but growing) number of theorists and theologians address animal issues within Christianity, and I will address this to a certain extent, the primary contemporary analysis involves the growth of blessing ceremonies for pets/animals in the late twentieth and early twenty-first centuries. Observations of blessings, interviews with people involved in organizing and promoting these ritual events, and analysis of this particular cultural phenomenon (limited to the United States in this study) are the focus, rather than the theological positions being written. These theological pieces are significant and open new horizons for thinking; thus I address some of these in depth, particularly contemporary theologies, in the final chapter. But I examine this increasingly popular ritual as an example of contemporary issues related to animals and Christianity. With this in mind I again refer to the methods of Jean-Claude Schmitt: "This enquiry is itself part of a broad current of research into 'popular literature', 'oral traditions', 'popular culture', 'popular religion' and so on. I do not propose, however, to survey the various and often contradictory approaches that these expressions cover, nor even to situate my own work in relation to them. My approach and methodology will become clear as I proceed with the analysis."[34]

Outline of the Study

The Mediterranean world of the Roman Empire and its many religious influences, from Judaism to Isis worship to traditional Roman religions (based on Greek traditions before them), gave rise to Christianity. So chapter 2, "Guardians of the Gateway," outlines the animal world of these many religious traditions, and of those traditions that influence Christianity as it spreads into Europe. Since religions never exist in a void or in isolation from myriad cultural influences, the place of animals in societies that shape Christianity obviously impacts the place of animals within Christianity. Meanings, symbols, and relationships between human-animals and nonhuman animals generate from this interplay of cultural constructions. So who is the lion in the Mediterranean world of the first century of the common era, and how did lions function religiously? Who is the dog in Greek mythology? What does it suggest when a religious tradition, as Christianity is in the early twenty-first century, holds ceremonies blessing pets while millions of animals die painful deaths and live excruciating lives in factory farms? Of course, answers to these questions are inevitably incomplete, but setting the context remains necessary. This section outlines each of the major historical periods of the two thousand years years during which Christianity has existed, arguable delineations of periods, of course, and offers major themes for animals and society in each of these historical/cultural contexts. Again, it is not and cannot be exhaustive; it is instead a sampling of animal-human relationships in each of the historical periods.

In chapter 3, "The Ephesian Lion and Clay Sparrow," I move to an analysis of animals in the earliest Christian texts, with glimpses into both the apocryphal texts that relate stories of apostles and martyrs and some early extracanonical gospels with alternative accounts of the life of Jesus. The prevalence of animals in these stories, as opposed to their relative absence in the canonical New Testament, is striking. Whether one encounters stories of the child Jesus in dialogue with a pride of lions or Paul working with a preaching dog, it is particularly telling that animals are, so often, connected directly to the earliest Christian heroes. Stories of the martyrs also shape much of the self-understanding of Christians for generations, arguably until the present. If animals are among the first martyrs, what does that mean for the anthropocentric Christianity that follows?

In chapter 4, "Counted Among the Saints," I move into the Middle Ages, addressing hagiographical and iconographical images of saints. I propose a four-pronged organization of animal-saint stories: animals as exemplars of piety, animals as sources of revelation, animals as saintly martyrs, and animals as the primary intimate other in relationship. Hagiographical accounts and visual texts provide material for this part of the study. Questions of animals as subject or object, as symbolic or real, arise throughout. This premodern time period is replete with accounts of animals as actors in Christian stories, quite distinct from the modern telling of Christian tales.

In the next chapter, "The Granted Image," I narrow the focus to two species—*Homo sapiens* (humans) and *Canis familiaris* (dogs). Dogs and humans formed a seemingly unique bond thousands of years ago, and this connection plays itself out in Christianity as well as in almost every other aspect of human (human-dog) culture. I contend that dogs are such a "granted image" that we often "take for granted" their omnipresence. Again, oral and visual texts tell the story, sometimes of dogs as holy, other times of dogs as heretical or even demonic. They function as both like us and other than us in myriad and complex ways.

Chapter 6, "Animals Return to the Sanctuary," analyzes a contemporary cultural phenomenon in the United States: blessings of pets/animals. In the last two decades of the twentieth century this seemingly "new" ritual infiltrated the Christian liturgical cycle throughout the United States (and in some other parts of the world, but space limits that complicated discussion). From the huge, annual gathering at the Cathedral of St. John Divine in New York City to small, interfaith blessings in local parks, early October (usually) marks the movement of animals into the sanctuary, or at least into the temporary sanctuary outside formal Christian buildings. The Feast of St. Francis, celebrated on October 4, is the preferred date for the blessings of "pets" or "animals" (a distinction that will be addressed in that chapter) because of that saint's connection to animals. Is this a move toward animals reentering the Christian sanctuary? If so, why?

Finally, in chapter 7, "Animals Are Good to Think," I draw some conclusions about where animals stand in Christianity in the early twenty-first Christian century based on newly arising theological discussions related to other-than-human animals and on the historical movement through the preceding chapters. As a prelude to the contemporary theological ideas, I examine the demise of the animal in Christianity by looking at the shifting philosophical and religious worldviews of the Reformation and the Enlightenment. "I think, therefore I am," proclaimed René Descartes (1596–1650), thus relegating other-than-human animals to a realm previously unimagined in Western, or any other, culture. A glance at the various religious discussions surrounding this, to a worldview that would no longer include anything but the human, and its impact on animals, moves the discussion to the present as the modern period is addressed, including its shift away from visual and legendary animal inclusion.

Andrew Linzey, Matthew Scully, Carol Adams, Jay McDaniel, and Stephen Webb are introduced as contemporary theologians who bring animals back into the center of Christian dialogue. The text ends where it began in some ways, asking if Christianity is, indeed, irredeemably speciesist.

Let me offer two examples of connections between the methods used in this study and the historical outline that runs through the remainder of the text. A feminist approach to history requires looking between the lines of texts, behind the lines of texts, and into the faces staring out from images. Why, in the Middle Ages, is the ass so unnoticed as an image in art? What happens when we take notice of asses and their stories? When one rethinks representational strategies and meanings, with the idea in mind that making animals purely and always symbolic leads to their very erasure from history, one must take their representation differently. This then leads, for example, to the noticing of dogs in images that span Christian history. Why are dogs everywhere? Are they just images of the heretic? Or might they be represented so often because they were subjects in the human story? For most generations of human history animals have been omnipresent, as they are today—with the exception that in contemporary U.S. culture humans are surrounded by dead animals in the form of meat more often than by live animals who have a subjectivity of their own. Another connection is made in the recognition of the amazing growth of a relatively new ritual, one that has not been acknowledged or analyzed by researchers in any significant way. This recognition poses the question of a reintroduction of animals into the religious realms from which they essentially have been excluded for generations. Though, on the other hand, it might simply reobjectify animals, just as modern zoos and circuses do.

Thus I plunge into this study of animals in the history of the Christian tradition with the hope that applying myriad methods and various gazes might illuminate something that has remained in the dark for too many years. Thinking about the presence of so many animals in this seemingly anthropocentric tradition might lead more people to a consideration of Albert Schweitzer's plea:

> No one must shut his eyes and regard as non-existent the suffering of which he spares himself the sight. Let no one regard as light the burden of his responsibility. While so much ill-treatment of animals goes on, while the moans of thirsty animals in railway trucks sound unheard, while so much brutality prevails in our slaughter-houses, while animals have to suffer in our kitchens painful death from unskilled hands, while animals have to endure intolerable treatment from guiltless men, or are left to the cruel play of children, we all share the guilt.[35]

2. Guardians of the Gateway

Shifting Historical Settings
for Christianity and Animals

I have taken good care of divine ibises, falcons, cats and dogs; I
have buried them according to ritual, I have covered them with
ritual oils [and] I have wrapped them in sacred cloths.[1]

Christianity grew out of the various religious traditions found in the Mediterranean world two thousand years ago, and its forms continue to shift, as
do those of all religions, based on constantly changing historical-cultural
settings. Even the singular designation of the tradition, "Christianity," rather
than a plural form, "Christianities," serves as a misnomer. Both the intertwined and diverse roots as well as the intertwined but hugely divergent
religion called Christianity is too varied to truly be thought of as only one
religion. Although I use both the singular and plural designations inter-
changeably, the complexity of the tradition guards against the assumption
of a unified position on any issue or history.

Judaism, mystery religions, myriad pagan traditions, and the quasi-official,
state religion of the Roman Empire, to name just a few, provided the primary sources for early forms of Christianity. As they develop, Christianities
incorporate various aspects of these traditions and their belief systems. By
the beginning of the twenty-first Christian century, the religious tradition,
literally in hundreds if not thousands of forms worldwide, had incorporated
capitalism into its ideology in insidious, subtle ways.[2] From this process a
rather uncertain place is forged for animals in Christian traditions. Each
of those ancient Mediterranean religious traditions, in their first-century
constructions, included and excluded animals in various manners, thus
influencing the foundations for the inclusion and exclusion of animals in
Christianities. The same pattern occurred through Western history; cultural
contexts influenced the place of animals in the religion. Thus, for example,

animals fill a different role in medieval Christianity from the role they fill in post-Enlightenment Christianity.

The discourse of text and context, both defined very broadly, are the key to the disciplines categorized as the "humanities" and, I would argue, all fields of study. As is the case with all religions, the texts and contexts of Christianity constantly mutate. As a religion in its infancy, its formative periods, Christianity grew up in the arms of a Jewish-Roman-Hellenistic-Mediterranean complex of cultures. Although initially a religion of resistance to worldly authorities, at least in some of its early forms, the history of Christianity intertwined with that of patriarchal and imperialistic Mediterranean and European powers, and thus the dominant forms of Christianity became increasingly anthropocentric. Animals and their stories ceased to have a significant voice in the Christian choir. During and after the scientific revolution and the Enlightenment, Christianity, along with the majority of interlocked European cultural systems, severed ties with the rest of nature. Alienation from any being other than the human, or the humanlike divine, set into these modern, dominant forms of Christianity. This intense, dualistic transformation, latent, or maybe apparent, throughout the history of Christianity, suppressed the holy animals within the religious tradition and its history with a kind of finality after the Enlightenment. Whereas the presence of animals had been integral to some aspects of various forms of Christianity in their earlier manifestations, the proclamations of such theologians and philosophers as René Descartes struck an apparent death knell for the efficacy and inclusion of animals in the circle of religious dialogue. Humans, ascendant for centuries, began to understand themselves as the only subjects worthy of divine consideration. All other animals were simply tools for human use.

Of course, this ranking of humans over animals, interlocked by myriad systems of oppression, traveled with European imperialism to the rest of the world, though some such human-animal hierarchies may have existed prior to this cultural contact. The binaries that place male over female, the constructed European "race" over all other constructed "races," and mind over body, just to name a few, connect directly to the ranking of humans over all (other) animals. Feminist and postcolonial theories suggest that as long as one of these systems of domination remains, none of them are truly subverted. Articulating the significant role that animals have played throughout the scope of Christian history might strengthen the process of ending the connected, reinforcing dominations. It also provides one of many perspectives that have the potential to influence the development of a renewed, biocentric Christianity.[3]

Within this broad historical context, then, what are some of the major cultural impacts on "animals and Christianity" throughout the religion's two thousand year lifespan? What did animals signify in the various traditions that formed Christianity in its infancy? What happens to animals in the Middle Ages as the tradition spreads into and eventually overtakes much of what was previously "pagan" Europe? And, then, what do the Enlightenment and scientific revolution mean for animals in Christianity as it struggles to adapt to these new humanisms? Finally, what of market capitalism's definitions of everyone and everything as a commodity?

This chapter takes a relatively broad sweep while trying to provide some specific images of the shape-shifting of animals throughout this cultural trajectory of Western forms of Christianity. I do not claim to offer an entire catalog of connections; rather, I suggest a glimpse that provides insight into these transformations and mutations of animals between the traditions in relationship to Christianity. From sacred ibises in Egypt to healing animals in pagan-becoming-Christian Europe to the animal as machine of Descartes and, finally, to the mass factory farming of animals in a U.S. culture that also begins blessing its pets in the twentieth Christian century, it is a complicated history, but understanding its framework is requisite if one is to understand animals within the religious worldview. This information should serve as a kind of background, the ocean in which specific animal-Christianity relations swim.

The Sacred World of the Mediterranean

Birds fly in the stone carvings, lions guard the entrance, and snakes wrap themselves gracefully around human figures on the facade of San Rufino Basilica in Assisi, Italy. This church served as a cathedral during the lifetime of Francis of Assisi, a saint whose hagiographical accounts relate his love of animals. It is no wonder that Francis included so many creatures in his images of heaven on earth; they surrounded him in both real and symbolic form at the parish church in which he was baptized. Many of the animals he saw each time he entered the cathedral, erected on top of a temple to Gaia (the earth goddess), occupied sacred positions in the Mediterranean for centuries.[4]

A few examples of Christianity's incorporation of animals and animal symbolism from other religions suffice to establish historical and cultural influence and syncretism during the first centuries of Christianity. Indeed, the early Mediterranean traditions have an impact, at the very least, on the symbolic role of animals in Christianity until the waning years of the Middle Ages. The list of traditions and animals is endless, from ancient Sumeria to Egypt and Palestine, and the complexity of animals within religious systems needs to be kept in mind. Philippe Germond and Jacques Livet explain this in their study of Egyptian religion and animals: "Driven by our modern obsession with classification and categorization at all costs, we would be happier if we could establish a neat distinction in Egyptian thought between 'animal deities' and 'sacred animals.' Is there a fundamental difference, for example, between the goddess Bastet's manifestations in the form of a cat-headed woman and her appearances in the guise of a cat pure and simple? . . . The distinction between animal god and sacred animal is not a neat and orderly one."[5] Animals are fluid, divine, symbolic, and real in these ancient traditions that include myriad animals. Therefore, I selected two animals that are particularly prominent as examples of relationships with Christianity—lions and asses—followed by a brief outline of the role of animals in two Mediterranean cultures that obviously had an impact on Christianity, the cultures of Egypt and Rome. Of course, as the religious traditions of Judaism influenced Christianity most directly, I address these connections in the following chapter.

Lions, long revered in Mediterranean religious and cultural traditions, retain that exalted role as they enter Christian liturgical space. A lion is the symbolic animal of the evangelist Mark and in this connection appears in most churches built and decorated with religious art prior to the Reformation. They also flank the doorways of sacred buildings, the thrones of religious elites, and the pedestals of gods and goddesses. Christianity retained this tradition for centuries (and many secular buildings follow suit in the contemporary world, as evidenced by places such as the New York Public Library).

Archaeologist Marija Gimbutas studied neolithic Europe for decades, focusing on the shift from "Old European" to "Proto-Indo-European" cultures.[6] Her basic theory suggests that equalitarian, indigenous (Old) Europeans were both assimilated and destroyed by invading, militaristic Proto-Indo-Europeans (Kurgans). Simultaneously, the fertility, goddess-based religions of Old Europe both syncretized with and, to a certain extent, were destroyed by the sky-god, afterlife-focused religions of the Kurgans. Gimbutas's research includes sites in present-day Bosnia, Macedonia, Greece, and Italy.

One of the key figures (c. 6000 BCE) she analyzes is a goddess flanked by two male felines. The goddess's ample body is positioned with her hands on the heads of the massive cats, their tails curling over her shoulders. Gimbutas points to similar representations in Minoan religion, such as the Mistress of Animals or Goddess of the Mountain flanked by lions (c. 1600 BCE).[7] Lions also serve as "guardians of the gateway" at the "lion's gate" of Mycenae (c. 1250 BCE) and at the temple near Ur in ancient Babylon (c. 2000 BCE).[8] So this common religious imagery spans literally centuries before Christianity and is retained by it.

In Egypt a recent discovery reconfirms theories about the prominence of lions in Egyptian sacred systems. Worship of Bastet, the feline goddess referenced by Germond and Livet, spread throughout Egypt with a cult center at Bubastis. Mummification of cats based on the worship of Bastet, and I would suggest based on the significance of cats in Egyptian culture as a whole, point to the influence of the cat goddess in Egypt. A lion, mummified and placed in the tomb of Maia, the wet nurse to King Tutankhamun, indicates that these other felines also held a some sacred position in Egypt. Some scholars suggest that as a male, "the mummified lion may have been considered as an incarnation of the god Mahes (Miysis), son of the goddess Sekhmet or Bastet. . . . Lions are thought to have been bred in sanctuary precincts and buried in a sacred necropolis."[9] The goddess Bastet, dozens of mummified cats, and now the mummified lion all point to the continuity of felines as sacred in the pre-Christian Mediterranean world. There are even connections to the highest god, Ra, who was sometimes addressed as "Supreme Tomcat." Early Egyptian mythologies indicate that this sun god, Ra, overcame darkness in the form of a giant cat.[10]

Evidence indicates that many ancient peoples, in addition to those mentioned above, had "lion cults," including the Hittites, Persians, Assyrians, and Babylonians. In a study of a procession in honor of the goddess Artemis, Lillian Lawler stresses this point: "From the earliest times, the lion was associated with divinity. Cook and Evans recognized lion-headed daemons, servants of the great mother goddess, in the art of pre-Hellenic Greece and Crete. These scholars concluded that in the prehistoric period there was an actual 'lion cult' in Greece, Crete and Asia Minor."[11] With this long history in mind, it makes sense that Christ is symbolized by Aslan, the lion, in C. S. Lewis's classic *The Chronicles of Narnia.*[12]

Lions emerge in stories throughout Christian history and in its earliest texts. From the lions in Daniel's den, to the lion baptized by Paul, to Aslan, these mighty animals enter the scene often. Significant encounters are mentioned in the following chapters. But it is telling that lions grace the entries of numerous Christian churches, including San Rufino in Assisi; they accompany saints, such as the storied Jerome; and they adorn the base of pulpits, such as the one carved by Pisano for the cathedral in Siena.

Another animal found in both ancient Mediterranean traditions and subsequently throughout the history of Christianity is the ass, a complex and extremely significant animal. Of course, the story of Balaam's ass in the Hebrew Bible (Numbers 22:21–35) is one of the most significant animal stories in the canonical texts. In that story the ass saw the angel of the Lord and the human did not. In early Christianity the ass displays both the dif-

Pulpit by Pisano, Duomo, Siena, Italy. Photo taken by author.

ferentiation of newly developing religion from official Roman religion and, simultaneously, the borrowing of images from classical traditions by some of the first Christian artists. Jesus' entry into Jerusalem on the back of a donkey is prominent in this early art, as is the ass, accompanied by a cow, attentively kneeling by the baby Jesus. The image contrasts with those of emperors and nobility, who enter in chariots or mounted on regal horses. Such contrast is deliberate, it seems, as the humility of Jesus is displayed.

But the ass was not always or only a symbol of the most humble. Helen Adolf suggests that asses declined in status because of the rise of the horse in the ancient world. Prior to that displacement, indications point to the ass as prominent, or at least more prominent than this maligned species has remained. So, for example, Queen Shubad in Ur had her team of asses buried with her, possibly for use in the afterlife.[13]

Simultaneously, the ass connects Christianity to Roman traditions. As Thomas Mathews states, "Early Christian art is rich with Dionysiac associations." He also points out that in "classical art the ass is common in Dionysiac processions, whether carrying Hephaistus, the divine smith, on his entry to Mt. Olympus, or Silenus, Dionysus' aged mentor. . . . In addition, a mule, offspring of an ass and a horse, is the common transport of Dionysus himself."[14] Thus just as visual portrayals show Jesus and Mary riding on an ass in the flight to Egypt (Matthew 2:14–15), so Dionysus mounts an ass rather than the more noble horse, making even more interesting connections to Christianity. Images of Jesus' entry into Jerusalem while riding an ass appear on numerous Roman sarcophagi, thereby reinforcing the connection of this humble animal to Jesus. Later, asses return to the scene in hagiographical accounts of saints, such as those of Anthony of Padua.

Early Christianity was influenced in some direct and some indirect ways by Egyptian religious traditions, which had impacted for centuries Greek and Roman religious traditions, as well as the traditions of the people of Israel. As stated above, felines play a prominent role in Egyptian religion and continue to function symbolically in Christianity; also, Jesus and Mary fled on an ass to Egypt. So this North African culture remained central in the life of early Christianity. Many early Christian communities and leaders hailed from Egypt, the home of some of the most ancient forms of the tradition. Certainly, the longstanding religions of Egypt were apparent to early Christian thinkers, such as Lactantius (c. 260–330 CE), who remained leery of their influence. In *The Divine Institutes,* Lactantius, a prolific writer and respected leader, refers directly to "the nation of the Egyptians, who worship the most disgraceful figures of beasts and cattle, and adore as gods some things which it is even shameful to speak of."[15]

Writers from the earliest Christian centuries, including those deemed most significant by later orthodoxy and labeled the Ante-Nicene Fathers, recognized that including animals in any official capacity within Christianity might smack of paganism, a category under which traditional Egyptian religious practices certainly fell during those centuries.[16] Arnobius, writing in the late third century CE, seems deeply aware of animals as integral to myriad familiar religious traditions. In his *Against the Heathens* he states, "Temples have been erected with lofty roofs to cats, to beetles, to heifers:—the powers of the deities thus insulted are silent; nor are they affected with any feeling of envy because they see the sacred attributes of vile animals put in rivalry with them."[17] Granted, however, Arnobius critiques any use of imagery as a direct correlation to the divine, including the human image: "You mock the mysteries of the Egyptians, because they ingrafted the forms of dumb animals upon their divine causes, and because they worship these very images with much incense, and whatever else is used in such rites: you yourselves adore images of men, as though they were powerful gods, and are not ashamed to give to these the countenance of an earthly creature."[18] So while critiquing Egyptian beliefs and practices, Arnobius also provides a parallel critique of some manifestations of early Christianity.

Certainly, the formative years of Christianity cannot be comprehended without a look at the influenced wielded by the world of the Roman Empire, a world in which animals did not usually fare well; then again, most human animals also fared poorly under this empire. Animals were sacrificed throughout the Roman Empire for ritual purposes. In his study *Spectacles of Death in Ancient Rome,* Donald Kyle outlines the many ways animals fit into the religious life of the empire:

> Moreover, in certain festivals . . . early Romans also hunted, baited or abused animals. In the Ludi Cereales, the games of the ancient Italian fertility goddess Ceres, dating from before 202 BC, foxes with burning brands tied to their tails were let loose in the Circus Maximus. Pliny mentions an annual sacrifice of dogs who were crucified live and carried about in a procession. In the Ludi Piscatorii fish from the Tiber were thrown live into a fire in the Forum. . . . Even before it expanded overseas, Rome brought dogs and wild beasts from the local countryside into the heart of the city and publicly tormented or hunted them.[19]

Particular sacrifices connected to the emperor and the games of the circuses often involved animals as well. For instance, some reports indicate that during celebrations on the accession of Caligula (12–41 CE) "160,000 victims were publicly sacrificed in the next three months, or even less time."[20] The numbers of animals killed in games held in the Roman Colosseum and in games throughout the empire escalated over time, with shocking statistics recorded: "the 9,000 beasts killed in AD 80 in Titus' games to dedicate the Flavian Amphitheater, the 10,000 gladiators who fought and 11,000 animals who were killed in Trajan's games of AD 108–9, or the 3,000 beasts in Probus' show in AD 281. . . . Art and literature suggest that, especially under the Empire, the victims killed in the greatest quantities were animals."[21] Many of these animals were imported, with certain exotic animals valued more highly than others. So, for example, "Pompey's games included the slaughter of 20 elephants, 600 lions, 410 leopards, various apes, the first north-European lynx to be seen at Rome, and the first rhinoceros."[22]

Eventually, possibly based on economic decisions more than moral ones, "venationes" (staged hunts) became more common than gladiatorial competitions.[23] I address the fascinating relationships between the animals killed in the arenas and early Christian martyrs in the next chapter, but all indications point to significantly more animal than human deaths in these settings, though certainly the numbers of humans killed was horrific. Some historians even suggest that certain species were driven to extinction by the various games of Rome: "Procurement of animals for the Roman arena . . . exhausted the hunting grounds of North Africa, where elephant, rhinoceros, and zebra became extinct. The hippopotamus and crocodile were banished from the lower Nile to upper Nubia. By the fourth century AD, a writer could lament that there were no elephants left in Libya, no lions in Thessaly, and no hippopotami in the Nile."[24] Of course, habitat destruction, competition from domesticated species, and depletion of fisheries added to the demise or deterioration of populations of species.

Other animals and cultural influences undoubtedly impact Christianity in its infancy. The bull was considered a sacred animal that challenged Israelite monotheism. This might indicate another connection to Egyptian traditions, particularly that of the Apis bull. According to Plutarch, "when it was the repository of the soul (ba) of the Ptah, the celebrated Apis bull was considered as a sacred animal, and otherwise it was worshipped as a divinity in its own right."[25] As indicated in the introduction, bulls still participate in Christian rituals, such as the Feast of San Zopito in Loreto Aprutino, Italy. In addition, fish figure prominently as symbols throughout the history of the tradition and "real fish" hear the word when Anthony of Padua preaches to them. The list of animals and influences continues, suggesting, in my opinion, an important impact on Christianity.

Pagan-Becoming-Christian Europe

Animals appear, disappear, and reappear as Christianity, ever so slowly, moves through Europe, syncretizing with and, in some ways, replacing the ancient traditions of the varied peoples inhabiting and moving around the Continent. The conversion-syncretization process happened over centuries and, arguably, Christianity never took hold completely everywhere in Europe. If one looks for overt signs and connects alternative European religious traditions that predate Christianity with witchcraft, for example, a sometimes problematic but also telling link, then paganism existed in pockets throughout Europe until the eighteenth century, when the last witchcraft trials and executions took place. By the early twenty-first century, neopaganism had emerged, claiming historical roots in these ancient traditions.[26] Yet Christianity did move into these diverse cultures, and as it did it transformed in significant ways to meld with certain aspects of the ancient religions of Europe.

At this point I pause to offer some definitions of a contested problematic concept—paganism—because of its natural connection, in the minds of many Westerners, to nature (ergo animals) and religion. Of course, this also begs the complex and shifting understandings of "nature" itself, as if humans are somehow not part of nature. Emperor Constantine issued the Edict of Milan in 313 CE, thus legalizing Chrisitanity and initiating the shift of religious power in the Roman Empire. "Pagan" developed, over the course of centuries, as a designation comprehensible only within the context of the institution of the church (not just the religion of Christianity) and of that institution in a position of power and control. In other words, a complex of other-than-Christian religious traditions were associated with this designation—Roman/Greek religions, nature-based (and varied) traditions of Europe, eventually traditions of almost anyone who was not Christian anywhere in the world (with the exception of Jews and sometimes Muslims, for a variety of historically complex reasons). The Latin roots of the word itself hail from distinctions between urban dwellers and rural folk; *pagus* is the countryside and *paganus* is a country-dwelling person. This could point to the early urbanization of Christianity and the eventual connection of paganism with those who connect the sacred with nature.[27] Eventually the term "pagan" signifies the other-than-Christian, usually nature-based, complex of religious traditions.[28]

During the sixth and seventh centuries, as missionaries embarked on treks throughout Europe, they encountered the continued strength of indigenous European religions: "In Saxony, sacrifices were regularly performed in forest sanctuaries. In Poitiers, sacrifices were offered on certain days of the year to a mountain lake, as people threw fabrics, cheese, wax, and bread into the water and feasted for three days. On the border between Frisia and Denmark, sacrifices were performed at a spring regarded as so sacred that nothing around it could be touched."[29] The actual policies of the church constantly shifted between accommodation, appropriation, and attempted destruction of pagan practices. So, for example, Pope Gregory I (540–604 CE, pope from 590) instructs King Ethelbert, and thus his missionaries to England, to "multiply the zeal of your uprightness in . . . conversion; suppress the worship of idols; overthrow the structures of the temples."[30] But within a short time period Gregory shifted positions and decided that the shrines should not be destroyed; rather, "the temples themselves are to be aspersed with holy water, altars set up in them, and relics deposited there."[31]

Various arguments suggest that some forms of paganism morphed into new aspects of Christianity whereas other aspects were directly appropriated. Certainly this is the case for numerous pagan temples that later become Christian churches, including the Pantheon in Rome and the Asklepieion at Athens. A fascinating study of this second site, the Asklepieion, traces at least three Christian basilicas built on the ruins of the pagan temple. The church included the site of the temple and also earlier sites, including the sacred spring. Evidence of overlap, in terms of both time and space, between pagan practices of healing and Christian appropriation and transformation of these practices and spaces is strong.[32]

In addition, stories that could be cited almost ad infinitum indicate connections between pagan and emergent Christian traditions in myriad legends of saints.[33] These hagiographical accounts, specifically the ones related to animals, are addressed in detail in a later chapter, but an example, still connected to healing, should be helpful at this juncture as well. Healing is central to many religious traditions for reasons too complex to address in this context, but it is integral to pagan European traditions and remains so in Christianizing Europe. So in addition to places, figures shift from pagan healers to healing saints. One collection of such healing saints emerges from Celtic Wales. Saint Gwenfrewi, a female Welsh saint from the sixth century, is usually associated with a curative shrine and a holy well. The well is documented as early as the eleventh century and remains a site of pilgrimage, a famous "curative shrine," in the twenty-first century. As a matter of fact, a number of Celtic saints preside over holy wells, including several associated to St. Columba.[34] Evidence suggests that these traditions, both wells and holy figures, may have been inherited from pagan Celtic spirits because wells "were the foci of pre-Christian curative ritual all over pagan Europe."[35]

These brief examples do an injustice to the complex process, occurring over centuries, through which Christianity became the dominant and, some would contend, only religion of Europe. While historians once assumed that Christianity, in some finalized Catholic form, controlled the European Middle Ages, that assumption no longer stands. Some scholars posit that pagan traditions never died and exist in the early twenty-first century as neopaganism.[36] Others suggest that throughout the Middle Ages, the population of parts of Europe is only "superficially Christianized."[37] Certainly, though, aspects of the ancient religious practices of myriad European cultures integrated into Christianity. As Van Engen states, "The end product was inevitably some synthesis between the old and new cultures under the aegis of Christendom. . . . Cultures do change, even oral and customary ones, and at some undeterminable point most people in Europe came to consider themselves 'Christian.' This transition, from one customary religious culture to another, can only have been very slow with much retained from the old and absorbed from the new."[38] So, what of animals and their shifting role as paganism merges into Christianity through the Middle Ages?

Since a later chapter deals entirely with saints and animals from this time period, I will wait to address that particular aspect of the response to the history. But the ambiguity of animals in the pagan-becoming-Christian Middle Ages is evident. This comes through clearly in Mathews's study of Christian art. Here he ties together early images with those that stretch into the Middle Ages:

The importance of the ass in Early Christian art signals a new attitude toward the whole animal kingdom. While the classical world sometimes drew moral lessons from animal behavior and made them act out human dramas in Aesop's Fables, the Christian mind saw them as somehow collaborators in the human endeavor, both in revealing the depths of God's mysterious plans and in helping people along on the treacherous road to salvation. Thus the whole realm of beasts and birds entered into the religious sphere. Medieval man expected to encounter a vision of Christ in the horns of a stag as readily as in any sanctuary. On the other hand if one's faith in the unfathomable mystery of the Eucharist should falter, an ass might lead the way to the altar and kneel devoutly to venerate the Sacrament.[39]

While animals are often associated with particular pagan practices, such as sacrifices to local deities, they remain central to Christian ideas, ideals, and hagiographies. So Christian leaders would simultaneously condemn practices that included animals while endorsing stories that praised their edifying virtues. I suggest that the Middle Ages, in part because of the continuing influence of popular religious practices that combined Christianity and pagan traditions, remained a time of relative inclusion for animals within the Christian tradition. Their presence persists and their stories fit naturally within the broader view of the tradition.

Miracle of the Mule by Vecchietta, baptistery, Siena, Italy. Photo taken by author.

That stated, theologians of the later Middle Ages, such as Thomas Aquinas (1225–1274), certainly consider human beings superior while still maintaining a place for other creatures. First, for Aquinas, the entirety of God's creation reflected divine glory:

> For he produced things into being in order that His goodness might be communicated to them; and because his goodness could not be adequately represented by one creature alone, he produced many and diverse creatures, that what was wanting to one representation of the Divine goodness might be supplied by another. For goodness, which in God is simple and uniform, in creatures is manifold and divided; and hence the whole universe together participates in the Divine Goodness more perfectly, and represents it better than any single creature whatever.[40]

For Aquinas, the variety in nature reflects the divine hand in creation. This coincides with other ideas from the same general time period, such as the moral lessons one could learn from animals. Yet in the Thomistic system, human superiority remains central and all other creatures attain their purpose only in relationship to humans: "Dumb animals and plants are devoid of the life of reason whereby to set themselves in motion; they are moved, as it were by another, by a kind of natural impulse, a sign of which is that they are naturally enslaved and accommodated to the uses of others."[41] Aquinas also posits that "charity does not extend to irrational creatures."[42] With this thirteenth-century ambiguity, animals showing the divine goodness on the one hand while not being worthy of human charity on the other, a shift in the place of animals in Christianity and European cultures as a whole seems evident. As becomes clear in the later chapter on animals and saints, animals most certainly deserved charity in the eyes of many saints, such as Giles, who protects a hind from hunters. Yet in the theology of Aquinas, humans moved closer to the divine and all other creatures began their descent.

Scientific Revolution, Reformation, and Enlightenment

> Who has ever seen any human beings kept under the control of animals, in such a way as we see everywhere herds of both wild and domesticated animals obeying men throughout their lives? Man not only rules the animals by force, he also governs, keeps and teaches them. Universal providence belongs to God, who is the universal cause. Hence man who provides generally for all things, both living and lifeless is a kind of god.[43]

With these words, Marsilio Ficino, a fifteenth-century Italian scholar and founder of the Platonic Academy in Florence, indicates a significant shift toward anthropocentrism in the history of Western Europe and, thus, of Christianity. While I deal with this more directly in a later chapter, the influence of the scientific revolution and Enlightenment on the place of animals in the history of Christianity cannot be overemphasized. As Ficino, Francis Bacon, and numerous other philosophers and theologians develop new ideological positions, accompanied by rapid shifts in technologies developed and implemented by humans, a "death of nature" occurred. As Carolyn Merchant states in her seminal book of that title, *The Death of Nature*, between "the sixteenth and seventeenth centuries the image of an organic cosmos with a living female earth at its center gave way to a mechanistic world view in which nature was reconstructed as dead and passive, to be dominated and controlled by humans."[44] Of course, theories regarding major shifts in Western culture and its perception of the place of human beings in relationship to the rest of nature as a result of the Enlightenment abound, as attested to by Merchant's study, but what is the direct impact of this transformation on animals?

Although numerous theologians conceive of a hierarchy placing humans above all other creatures throughout the generations of Christianity up to that point (the Great Chain of Being), animals still existed as subjects in some sense (a theory I propose throughout this text). But the scientific revolution and Enlightenment impact other-than-human animals in ways never before considered. Their ontological status shifts drastically, and thus their position within Christianity, though never particularly lofty, decreases concurrently. This shift expresses itself in particularly dramatic ways in the areas of confluence between Enlightenment philosophies and scientific discoveries or changes. As stated clearly by Max Oelschlaeger in his work on environmental history, *The Idea of Wilderness,*

> Perhaps no aspect of Modernism has had a greater effect on the idea of wilderness than science. . . . Galileo's new science, Bacon's new logic, Descartes's mechanistic reductionism, and Newton's physics are central to our study. Collectively they represent a *paradigm shift* so radical that the very meaning of the word *nature* was changed. . . . Nature is now believed to be the object of scientific study, and nothing remains in it of anything that is identifiably wilderness. . . . The modern mind has come to view nature as nothing more than matter-in-motion, whether planets, projectiles, or even animals.[45]

"Even animals" became objects reducible to scientific study, an idea shared by most Enlightenment philosophers: "The loss of memory is a transcendental condition for science. All objectification is a forgetting."[46] Such a forgetting of relationship forged the possibilities for scientific experimentation and exploitation of animals.

So, for example, when writing his description of the human body, Descartes makes it clear that the bodies of other animals have no intrinsic value. Referring to an English physician "called Harvey," probably Descartes' contemporary, William Harvey, who discovered the circulation of blood, Descartes speaks of an experiment geared toward understanding the heart's movement.[47] Descartes states, in a matter-of-fact manner, that Harvey "could have supported this last point by a very striking experiment. If you slice off the pointed end of the heart in a live dog, and insert a finger into one of the cavities, you will feel unmistakably that every time the heart gets shorter it presses the finger, and every time it gets longer, it stops pressing it."[48] Obviously, the beating heart of the live dog, who would obviously be in agony and would then die as a result of this experiment, held little or no value in comparison to the experiment itself.

Another overarching figure of the period, Francis Bacon, captured the changing role of animals, literally, in his descriptions of scientific research from *The New Atlantis,* Bacon's image of utopia. Merchant points out that Bacon's utopia, unlike those offered by several other philosophers, maintains a hierarchical and patriarchal social structure. His "nonegalitarian philosophy" extended to animals:[49]

We have also parks and enclosures of all sorts of beasts and birds, which we use not only for view or rareness but likewise for dissections and trials, that thereby we may take light [i.e., enlightenment] what may be wrought upon the body of man. Wherein we find many strange effect; as continuing life in them, though divers parts, which you account vital, be perished and taken forth; resuscitating of some that seem dead in appearance; and the like. We try also all poisons and other medicines upon them, as well of chirurgery, as physic. By art likewise, we make them greater or taller than their kind is; and contrariwise dwarf them, and stay their growth: we make them more fruitful and bearing than their kind is; and contrariwise barren and not generative. Also we make them differ in colour, shape, activity, many ways.[50]

Bacon's description provides an almost prophetic announcement of twenty-first-century genetic engineering.

But this position follows directly on Descartes' overall philosophical position regarding the relationship between "man and beast." In his *Discourse on Method* Descartes offers two significant differences:

For it is quite remarkable that there are no men so dull-witted or stupid—and this includes even madmen—that they are incapable of arranging various words together and forming an utterance from them in order to make their thoughts understood; whereas there is no other animal, however perfect and well-endowed it may be, that can do the like. This does not happen because they lack the necessary organs, for we see that magpies and parrots can utter words as we do, and yet they cannot speak as we do: that is, they cannot show that they are thinking what they are saying. . . . [T]his shows not merely that the beasts have less reason than men, but that they have no reason at all. . . . Nor should we think, like some of the ancients, that the beasts speak, although we do not understand their language. . . . It proves rather that they have no intelligence at all, and that it is nature which acts in them according to the disposition of their organs. In the same way a clock, consisting only of wheels and springs, can count the hours and measure time more accurately than we can with all our wisdom.[51]

At this point Descartes makes the move to animals as machines. This philosophical movement allows for an ethical system to support the growing scientific experimentation and technological advancements of the seventeenth and eighteenth centuries. It is the rise of the human to the spheres previously inhabited only by the divine. Humans are other than the rest of the creation, the rest of nature. Humans alone possess intelligence, a soul, and the ability to use words.

Thomas Hobbes (1588–1679) follows this same line of argument when he states that "speech or language" is "peculiar to man." Only humans know that "words are constituted by the will of men for the purpose of signification."[52] This last movement, to humans as language makers and signifiers, dovetailed well with the rise of the significance of the spoken and written (printed) word in Protestant Christianity in Europe.

Certainly the fifteenth to seventeenth centuries marked significant change in the philosophical and scientific worlds of Europe, but the above-mentioned connections, however direct or indirect they might be, with the growth of Protestantism cannot be overlooked. When the Protestant Reformation began, officially in 1517, the foundation of European religion shook to the core. And it should be no surprise that several emerging Protestant theologians had something to say about the relationship between the divine and humans and other animals. Martin Luther (1483–1546) and John Calvin (1509–1564), the two reformers whose names usually rise to the surface first, included animals in their theological systems. However, in both cases, animals seem to function less as subjects themselves and more as reflections of divine immanence and human dominion.

Scott Ikert offers an interesting study of Luther's lectures on Genesis. He suggests that Luther views animals as subject to Adam's fall; just as humans lose paradise, so do animals. While humans still held total dominion over other animals prior to the Fall, at least it was a benevolent dominion. Whereas "fullness of joy and bliss" marked Adam's relationship to "all the animal creatures," after the Fall humanity's exercise of dominion is "utterly beyond repair."[53] Following the Flood, human dominion shifts as animals "are made subject to man for the purpose of serving him even to the extent of dying." For Adam "it would have been an abomination to kill a little bird for food," but Luther contends "because the Word is added, we realize that it is an extraordinary blessing that in this way God has provided the kitchen with all kinds of meat."[54] Luther also makes several interesting observations regarding dogs, but those are addressed in a later chapter.

Calvin's references to animals proceed along the same general lines. While Peter Huff argues that Calvin has a "fascination with the animal kingdom," their primary purpose is to guide the human mind to God.[55] Animals exist not to glorify God in their own right but to benefit humankind in our contemplation, so Calvin describes them as "witnesses and messengers" because God "hath made the whole world for us." And not only the world but also the entire universe "was established especially for the sake of mankind."[56] Indeed, as Huff also points out, for Calvin "the most effective form of insult was comparison with the animal world."[57] It should also be noted, however, that in the Genevan theocracy established by Calvin, citizens were required "to take care of . . . animals" and were even allowed to miss Sunday worship for that purpose.[58] So the ambiguous and precarious position of animals continues in the world of early Protestant theology and ethics.

The story is incomplete, however, without brief mention of those who criticized the relegation of animals to the category of machine. In his *Dictionnaire philosophique* Voltaire (1694–1778) found it "pitiful" and an indication of "poverty of mind" for Descartes and others "to have said that the animals are machines deprived of understanding and feeling."[59] Jeremy Bentham (1748–1832), an English moral philosopher, penned a line that later became central to animal rights discourse. His philosophies offer a blanket critique of Descartes, Bacon, Ficino, and all those who follow in their footsteps. Bentham's commonly quoted statement, one that arguably grounds much of the modern animal rights movement, expresses the shift in humanity's relationship with and understanding of animals that he proposed: "The question is not, Can they reason? nor, Can they talk? but, Can they suffer?"[60]

The complexity of the period of the Enlightenment in Europe, with all of its religious and political turmoil, cannot be comprehended in just a few pages. But in its midst the earth and all of the species inhabiting the earth, except for humans, became part of the mechanical and technological order. As the masters and possessors of nature, including other animals, humans became the measure of all things religious, ethical, and moral.[61] With the rise of Protestant Christianity and its accompanying theological considerations, animals did indeed leave the sanctuary.

Animals in Twenty-first-Century European-U.S. Culture

[T]here is no "magical" essential difference between humans and
other animals, biologically speaking. (Charles Darwin)[62]

The word "speciesism" entered the vocabulary of Euro-American culture in the late twentieth century, first appearing in a privately funded pamphlet titled *Speciesism* written by Richard Ryder in 1970 and distributed in Oxford, England."[63] Ryder referenced Darwin's argument quoted above. Just as racism and sexism were examined as inherent aspects of patriarchal, hierarchicial, militaristic cultures, so speciesism became part of the dialogue. But it is not a widely accepted voice in philosophical, cultural, religious, and political conversations. Actually, it is a rather controversial voice at times, one that is denied by those who otherwise champion human rights. Marjorie Spiegel points to this controversy directly in the opening lines of her study *The Dreaded Comparison,* noting that "many people might feel that it is insulting to compare the suffering of non-human animals to that of humans."[64] Still, speciesism has reared its head and entered the dialogue.

In the 1970s several works were published in philosophical circles raising the specter of speciesism, primarily in the form of animal rights language: Stanley and Rosalind Godlovitch's *Animals, Men and Morals* (1972), Peter Singer's *Animal Liberation: A New Ethics for our Treatment of Animals* (1975), and Stephen Clark's *Moral Status of Animals* (1977). These initial works were followed by numerous analyses from the perspectives of moral philosophy and of theology by Andrew Linzey, Tom Regan, Jeanne Williams, Carol Adams, Michael Allen Fox, and others. But the realization among philosophers that humans are not the center of everything has had little impact on the consumer culture of late-twentieth- and early-twenty-first-century Euro-American culture. Again, while the entire time period cannot be examined in this brief space, one example of the ambiguity of animals in contemporary culture should suffice: the growth of animal rights political positions and ideologies in the midst of the exponential growth of the factory farming of animals.

Factory or industrial farming became the status quo for the production of animals as food during the last decades of the twentieth century in the United States. The process began after World War II, when intensive ("confinement") animal production commenced. Practices included keeping animals indoors and processing their lives through machinery rather than through human contact.[65] By the early 1960s critiques of these new intensive animal farming techniques appeared. Ruth Harrison's *Animal Machines,* published in 1964, employed the phrase "factory farming" for the first time. Her book explained, or rather exposed, the conditions of veal calves, pigs, and chickens in these new industrial farms.[66] A series of critiques followed Harrison's and continue to be published into the early twenty-first century.[67]

Of course, different interests state different positions. Those involved with the factory farming of animals conclude that such production is requisite to feed a growing human population and thus the condition of the animals is, basically, irrelevant. As a matter of fact, agricultural organizations, via promotional materials, tell the consuming public that industrial farming techniques are "beneficial for animal welfare" and "not harmful to the environment."[68] Those involved with animal welfare conclude that basic levels of humane treatment must be legislated and enforced, emphasizing that factory farming focuses on profit rather than humane treatment of animals. Others involved with radical animal rights movements call for an end to factory farming altogether. A type of middle ground was achieved in Britain in 1979, when the government established the Farm Animal Welfare Council. The council issued these codes to "provide animals with the new five freedoms":

Freedom from thirst, hunger, and malnutrition.
Freedom from thermal or physical distress (appropriate comfort and shelter).
Freedom from disease or injury.
Freedom to display most normal patterns of behavior.
Freedom from fear.[69]

Legislation in the United States, however, has not been forthcoming. Usually humans are excluded from prosecution for "cruelty to animals" if "animal husbandry or farming practice involving livestock" is part of the equation.[70]

While reciting the conditions of industrial farms seems tedious to some, most people ignore the conditions described by animal rights advocates. Michael Fox, a well-known scholar and activist, offers a succinct description:

For those not familiar with the bioethical travesties of conventional livestock production, the following concerns will provide a brief introduction. Extreme confinement and animal suffering: veal calves and sows unable to walk or turn around; laying hens confined to "battery" cages, 4–5 birds living in a space too small for even one to stretch her wings; dairy cows and beef cattle confined to dirty feedlots with no access to pasture and often no shade or shelter. . . . Widespread use of antibiotics and other drugs to control stress-related diseases and to stimulate growth, egg and milk production, with consequential consumer health risks from drug residues and the development of antibiotic resistant strains of bacteria responsible for food epidemics.[71]

One need only scan the websites of the Humane Society of the United States, People for the Ethical Treatment of Animals, and Farm Sanctuary, to name just a few, in order to see firsthand the conditions of animals on factory farms.

Carol Adams connects this process to the assembly-line culture introduced by Henry Ford and developed throughout the U.S. economy. She quotes Ford's autobiography, *My Life and Work,* in which he attributes the idea of assembly-line production to "the overhead trolley that the Chicago packers use in dressing beef." Another book on meat production suggests the same concept and process: "The slaughtered animals, suspended head downward from a moving chain, or conveyor, pass from workman to workman, each of whom performs some particular step in the process. . . . So efficient has this procedure proved to be that it has been adopted by many other industries." Adams continues with her own analysis of the assembly line production of animals for meat: "One of the basic things that must happen on the disassembly line of a slaughterhouse is that the animal must be treated as an inert object, not as a living, breathing being."[72]

So what is the ambiguity? By the late twentieth century U.S. forms of capitalism and production, including the production of animals for consumption, had spread to the entire globe.[73] But this rise of the inhumane treatment of billions of animals comes at the same time that specieisism, as a concept, is introduced and at the same time that animal welfare organizations and animal rights advocates, such as Peter Singer, take center stage in myriad discussions. There is a moral and pragmatic ambiguity at play in terms of the place of humans in relationship to other species. Throughout the United States, cities applaud their own efforts to reduce the numbers of homeless companion animals (mostly dogs and cats) killed in shelters, largely due to effective sterilization programs. Simultaneously, the number of food animals (cows, pigs, chickens) slaughtered after short and miserable lives rises every year. As I describe later, animals reenter Christian sanctuaries through blessing ceremonies, yet at these very ritual events no mention is made of farm animals and their situation.

The ambiguity persists. The same people who volunteer countless hours at their local humane societies mindlessly stop at the grocery store on the way home to purchase boneless, skinless chicken breasts manufactured without thought to the humane treatment of the chicken. Maybe the contemporary state of the relationship between humans and other animals could have been prophesied; it is based on a long series of complicated and tenuous connections. Over the centuries animals have been cursed and blessed, worshiped and eaten, sacrificed and sanctified. The often irrational and confusing trends of the society as a whole play themselves out in equally stressed fashions throughout the history of the Christian tradition.

3. The Ephesian Lion and Clay Sparrows

Animals in the Christian Canon
and Early Apocryphal Traditions

> And whatever he wills he can do: making dumb things to speak; he
> made Balaam's ass speak to him when he beat it; and a dog to say to
> Simon: "You are called for by Peter!" For Paul when he preached,
> he caused mules to speak of him: he made a lion speak to the
> people with God-given voice.[1]

Though Christianity indisputably focuses on humans, the presence of animals
is pervasive, even in the earliest of Christian texts. The apostle Paul engages
animals, particularly lions, and includes at least one in the sacrament of baptism; the sayings of Jesus refer to animals only occasionally but in significant
ways; early martyrs are both saved and destroyed by animals; and the "church
fathers" refer to animals throughout their writings. As is the case over the
entire stretch of Christian history, animals fare both well and poorly at the
hands and in the stories of early Christianity; but just as unquestionably as
they are assumed hidden or missing, they are visible when one looks.

Christianity in its various forms relies heavily on its sacred textual traditions. From those groups who understand themselves to be biblical "literal-
ists" to those who understand themselves as interpreters of sacred texts in
historical and cultural contexts, one of the few things that most, though not
all, Christians worldwide agree upon is the centrality of the Bible.[2] Consen-
sus on the most accurate versions and translations of these texts, and more
complicated still, the appropriate interpretations of them, never has been
and never will be achieved. Yet it is obvious that the canonical texts must
be taken into account for a complete study. Thus any position, argument, or
historical examination of the traditions of Christianity lacks inexcusably if
the Bible is not addressed.

That stated, for the purposes of this study I will not delve into animals in
the Christian canon in detail because this subject is treated effectively, though

not yet comprehensively, in other recent sources. Rather, a brief overview of some of the stories and texts provides the requisite foundation to the overall Christian animal story. The reader is also directed to a variety of complete and informative sources on animals in the sacred texts of Christianity.[3]

But I do examine animals in the apocryphal traditions and in other early Christian literature and hagiography from the first several centuries of the Christianity, literature that has not been addressed at all in some cases, or at least not to the extent of the canonical texts. This apocryphal literature lingers on the edges of modern Christianity, unfamiliar even to many of the most literate, progressive, and interested twenty-first-century Christians.[4] As stated by Bart Ehrman, those "who are interested in earliest Christianity are, as a rule, poorly informed concerning this literature; as a result, very few people, outside the ranks of the professional scholar, realize the diverse character of the religion in its earliest period."[5] But for some much earlier generations of Christians, the extracanonical stories of the apostles and martyrs were part of their religious world. Embracing or, at the least, refamiliarizing Christianity with some of its own texts aids in the process of remembering animals before they disappeared from the religious tradition. The same phenomenon occurred with the figure of Mary Magdalene as she reemerged in both research and popular stories based on Nag Hammadi texts in the late twentieth century.[6] So introducing these apocryphal texts to broader audiences, with a focus on the animals in them, provides alternative and oftentimes quite radical images of Christianity in its earliest manifestations.

Overview of Animals in the Canonical Scriptures

> Do not give what is holy to dogs; and do not throw your pearls
> before swine. (Matthew 7:6)

Dogs and pigs land on the bottom of many piles in the Christian canon. Swine drown in the sea when Jesus transfers the demons from the Gerasene man to the pigs' bodies, over two thousand of them in the Gospel of Mark, though the story is paralleled in slightly different versions in all three synoptic Gospels (Mark 5:1–13; Matthew 8:28–34; Luke 8:26–39). Of course, turning "men" into pigs occurs in other texts from the ancient Mediterranean world, most notably in Homer's *Odyssey*, when Circe, with a stroke of her wand, makes Ulysses' crew into pigs, though with their human memories intact. In the Hebrew scriptures that later become the Christian Old Testament, pigs bear the label of "unclean," along with numerous birds and a number of animals that live in the water (Deuteronomy 14).

Dogs are equally reviled, albeit for different reasons. In the description of the holy city in the book of Revelation, dogs are left outside the gates (Revelation 22:15), thus symbolically excluded from heaven. Jesus also questions the worthiness of dogs to receive scraps from the table, though he is challenged and, some would argue corrected, by the Syrophoenician woman (Luke 7:24–29). Dogs, in this instance, are a symbol for the other but also function as real dogs who do eat scraps from human tables.

Yet animals sometimes serve as divine agents in biblical stories. Two examples, from which numerous hagiographical stories referenced later most likely derive, are particularly relevant. 1 Kings 17 relates the story of the prophet Elijah's escape into the wilderness to hide from the evil king Ahab. According to the biblical account, the Lord sends him east of the Jordan River and tells him, "You shall drink from the brook, and I have commanded the ravens to feed you there." Elijah goes, and just as he was told, "the ravens brought him bread and meat in the morning, and bread and meat in the evening" (1 Kings 17:6). This theme of animals, oftentimes birds, providing food for holy ones in the wilderness recurs throughout Christian story and will be referenced in later chapters.

A second example is the well-known story of Daniel in the lion's den. Daniel, sealed in the den of hungry lions by a distressed King Darius, survived the night and proclaimed, "My God sent his angel and shut the lions' mouths, and they have not hurt me, because I was found blameless before him." Of course, that's not the case for Daniel's accusers, who "were brought and thrown into the den of lions . . . they, their children, and their wives; and before they reached the bottom of the den the lions overpowered them and broke all their bones in pieces" (Daniel 6:17–24). Early stories of Christian martyrs thrown to Roman lions repeat this template as well. Intertextuality is obviously at play as the stories of Christian martyrs parallel the stories of the sacred scriptures and figures.

So sometimes animals are cursed, such as the dogs and pigs, whereas other times they serve as divine agents, as do the raven and the hungry lions who spare Daniel and proceed to demolish his accusers. They can even provide a mouthpiece for God, as does Balaam's ass in another famous biblical story (Numbers 22). Here the "Lord opened the mouth of the donkey," who saved her human master, Balaam. In the midst of this story it could even be argued that Balaam, by striking his donkey three times, committed a sin. Certainly, the ass responds to Balaam as would an "aggrieved [human] worker."[7] Discounting the serpent in Genesis, however, Balaam's she-ass is the only animal who speaks in the Hebrew Bible.

Overall, there is little consistency in biblical references to animals. God blesses them and calls them good in the creation stories of Genesis 1 then subjects them to human domination a few verses later, though interpretations of these verses remains debated. God even seems to elevate humans above other animals when God asks Abraham to sacrifice his son Isaac but then saves Isaac by sending a ram to replace him on the sacrificial altar (Genesis 22). Various animals, including most prominently the lamb, serve as sacrifices to the divine throughout the Hebrew and Christian scriptures. Arguably, Christianity ends this practice of ritual animal sacrifice, replacing it with the sacrifice of Jesus, who then takes on the symbolic and actual role of the lamb. Since these texts were written by and are continually interpreted by humans, it makes a certain amount of common sense, on the part of humans, to include a concept of divinely ordained human power. Why not move toward species privilege and delineating humanity from other species, particularly in the unique human-divine relationship? It is, after all, in the interest of humans, at least in the short term.

The ambiguity continues throughout the texts as God saves animals by piling them onto Noah's ark, though multitudes of animals both human and nonhuman, die a violent, watery death at the same time according to this account. Then God changes the human diet from a vegetarian one (Genesis 1:29) to a carnivorous one (Genesis 9:3).[8] Throughout the Hebrew scriptures the integration of animals as an aspect of everyday life is apparent, but they are never included as direct members of the people of God, the nation of Israel. Throughout the New Testament Jesus employs animals in reference to God's love for humans; thus if God loves the sparrows, God loves humans even more. Scripture is ambivalent at best and thus lends itself to vastly differing interpretations. It is to several of these recent interpretations I now turn.

In his in-depth study of four words from the canonical Gospel of Mark, Richard Bauckham presents a fascinating reinterpretation of Mark 1:13: Jesus was "with the wild animals." First, while others might discount four words as irrelevant, Bauckham reminds the reader that Mark is a concise text, "no words are wasted."[9] Also, contrary to many readings of this text, wild animals are not portrayed as demonic; only Satan is. Jesus is in the wilderness with Satan, the wild animals, and the angels, but these are three distinct categories of beings. Satan is "the natural enemy of the righteous person and can only be resisted," angels "are the natural friends of the righteous person," and wild animals "are more ambiguous: they are enemies of whom Jesus makes friends."[10] In his thoughtful analysis, Bauckham places this text in the intertextual context of the Creation and the Fall, the introduction of the "fear" of humans by animals (Gen 9:2), and the idea that the "righteous and the wicked enjoy different kinds of relationships (beneficial for the righteous, detrimental to the wicked) to other beings."[11] In the brief passage from Mark, Jesus, as the messianic son of God, establishes the messianic peace with wild animals, thus redefining concepts of human dominion that exploit animals: "The animals are not said to fear him, submit to him, or serve him. The concept of human dominion over the animals as domination for human benefit is entirely absent. The animals are treated neither as subjects nor as domestic servants. . . . Jesus does not terrorize or dominate the wild animals, he does not domesticate them, nor does he even make pets of them. He is simply 'with them.'"[12] This radical reading is historically and textually rigorous, not reading the text through the lens of a contemporary ecological crisis but retrieving "another perspective."[13]

Andrew Linzey, one of the most prominent contemporary constructive theologians addressing animal issues in Christianity, interprets several canonical New Testament texts as indicative of his position that "to stand for Jesus is to stand for the Christ-like innocence of animals." Linzey notes that Jesus' ministry began "with the wild beasts" and that his entry into Jerusalem was "on the back of a beast of burden." Furthermore, he suggests that the identification of Jesus as "the Lamb of God" compares Christ "to a humble and unprotected animal."[14]

After reading the canonical scriptures, then, one is left uncertain about the status of animals. Sacrifice, witness of the divine, food, companion, enemy, unworthy, slightly more worthy, beloved by the Creator, clean and unclean— all of these designations apply to animals in the Christian canonical texts. But these ambiguous passages are not the only ones from the earliest strata of Christianity that address the issue of animals or that include accounts of animals as actors. The "other" stories recount differently the role of the "others."

Tell Me the (Other) Stories of Jesus

> And when Jesus was three years old, and when he saw boys playing, he began to play with them. And he took a dry fish and put it in a basin, and ordered it to breathe, and it began to breathe. And he said again to the fish, "Reject the salt which you have, and go into the water," and so it came to pass. (Infancy Gospel of Thomas, Latin text)[15]

The Gospels of Matthew, Mark, Luke, and John, the four evangelists symbolized by the eagle, the ox, the lion, and the "human/angel," claim priority over all other stories of Jesus, at least if one attends to the proclamations of the hierarchical church after it became the religious wielder of power for the Roman Empire. Certainly, traditions that predate the fourth century CE claim the authority of these four Gospels over all others, but myriad gospels shaped early Christianity. Often images with which most Christians are very familiar, such as the ox and the ass at the manger in the nativity stories, come from extracanonical accounts (neither the ox nor the ass is mentioned in Matthew or Luke, the two canonical Gospels that include stories of the birth of Jesus, but a visual image of the nativity is rarely without these two central figures). Although animals are not prominent in either the canonical or the extracanonical gospels, powerful stories emerge from the relatively unknown extracanonical traditions. It is helpful to examine several of these, after which I suggest an interpretation of them from the perspective of the role of other-than-human animals.

The Infancy Gospel of Thomas, the earliest versions of which were probably written in Greek or Syriac in the fourth century, tells the stories of Jesus after his birth through the age of twelve. These fascinating tales suggest what a truly "human" little boy with truly "divine" powers might do, such as kill another little boy who annoys him or resurrect the father of his friend. A few animals also enter the scenes. At the beginning of this section I quote from a Latin version of this text, a portion that tells the story of the young Jesus resurrecting a fish. The fish is already dried and cured with salt, but Jesus orders it to breathe and to deny the salt. In another account, Jesus molds clay pigeons on the Sabbath, something that is unlawful. When Joseph, his father, comes to scold him, Jesus claps his hands, brings the clay to life, and "the sparrows took flight and went away chirping."[16] More directly, in a Greek version of the gospel, Jesus says to the sparrows, "Go, fly away, and remember me while you live."[17] In both cases Jesus gives new life to animals, not just to humans. And in both cases divine power is obvious. The fish is resurrected, something only God can do, and the clay birds allude to the creation stories and the ability of God to breath life into creatures, including humans, crafted from the soil. Still, following in the ambiguity of the tradition as a whole, Jesus also kills at least one animal according to this gospel. A "viper" bites James and Jesus both heals James and kills the snake.

Another group of stories about the birth and early years of Jesus come from the Gospel of Pseudo-Matthew, a book closely connected to the Infancy Gospel of Thomas. This particular text might have been composed at a relatively late date, maybe the eighth century. But the imagery in it is striking. First, this is the text in which the ox and ass are found at the manger:

> And on the third day after the birth of our Lord Jesus Christ, Mary went out of the cave and, entering a stable, placed the child in the manger, and an ox and an

ass adored him. Then was fulfilled that which was said by Isaiah the prophet, "The ox knows his owner, and the ass his master's crib." Therefore, the animals, the ox and the ass, with him in their midst incessantly adored him. Then was fulfilled that which was said by Habakkuk the prophet, saying, "Between two animals you are made manifest."[18]

With intertextual references to Isaiah 1 and Habakkuk 3, this account of the nativity scene place other animals in a central position. They not only adore the infant but also, to a certain extent, verify his identity. But even more amazing encounters with animals follow as Jesus and his parents head across the desert. First, the reader hears that "lions and panthers adored him and accompanied them in the desert. . . . [T]hey showed their submission by wagging their tails, they worshipped him with great reverence." Though the animals initially frighten Mary, Jesus (still an infant) looks at her and says, "Be not afraid, mother, for they come not to do you harm, but they make haste to serve both you and me."[19] The language is still that of "service," thus dominion and hierarchy. However, it is at least a language of relationship in some form, rather than fear.

Nativity by Botticelli, Florence, Italy. Photo taken by author.

The infant Jesus has a definite connection to animals in the wilderness and, as prophesied in Isaiah 65, even shapes the animals' relationships with each other: "And the lions kept walking with them, and with the oxen and the asses and the beasts of burden, which carried what they needed, and did not hurt a single one of them, though they remained with them; they were tame among the sheep and the rams which they had brought with them. . . . They walked among wolves and feared nothing; and not one of them was hurt by another. . . . There were two oxen and a wagon in which they carried their necessities, and the lions directed them in their path." This passage indicates a certain transformation of the animals in Jesus' midst, and it could be a questionable one. Some theologians have criticized the prophesy of Isaiah, that the wolf will feed with lambs and the lion and the ox will eat together (see Isaiah 65:25). Is this a way of suggesting that all animals should be domesticated rather than accepting animals as "real"? Are they too much "symbol" and too little "reality" in these images in which carnivores and their prey live without one becoming food for the other? The image is one of the "peaceable kingdom."[20]

The peaceable kingdom imagery continues in the Gospel of Pseudo-Matthew in a second part (the "Pars Altera"). This is one of the stories of Jesus' childhood that fills in the gap between his infancy and the last several years of his life, gaps left intact when one relies solely on the canonical texts. In this account Jesus is going out of Jericho to the Jordan River on a frequently traveled road. On the route was "a cave where a lioness was nursing her whelps; and no one was safe to walk that way." But Jesus walked to the cave anyway, in the sight of many onlookers. The lions recognized him: "And when the lions saw Jesus, they ran to meet him and worshipped him. And Jesus was sitting in the cavern and the lion's whelps ran round his feet, fawning and playing with him. And the older lions, with their heads bowed, stood at a distance and worshipped him and fawned upon him with their tails." The people thought he had met his death in the cave with the lions until, suddenly, Jesus emerged from the cave with the lions before him and the cubs playing at his feet. Jesus then said to the people who had gathered, "How much better are the beasts than you, seeing that they recognize their Lord and glorify him; while you men, who have been made in the image and likeness of God, do not know him! Beasts know me and are tame; men see me and do not acknowledge me." Jesus then crosses the Jordan with all the lions, bids them, "Go in peace," and instructs them to hurt no one. Significantly, he also says, in the hearing of the people, "[N]either let man injure you." Basically, Jesus gave the lions safe passage.[21] Rather than kill these lions, who had moved into areas inhabited by humans, Jesus facilitates their return to the wilderness. He also displays the faithfulness of the lions to the crowds of humans gathered to witness these events.

Thus even as a child Jesus takes other animals seriously. They should be allowed to live in peace, away from the fear and violence of humans. They are brought into the "peaceable kingdom" prophesied in connection with the Messiah. Traditional Christian theology posits that the Fall caused a rift for the entire creation. This interpretation likely derives in large part from Paul, who in his letter to the Romans, states that "the creation was subjected to futility. . . . [T]he creation itself will be set free from its bondage to decay and will obtain the freedom of the glory of the children of God" (Romans 8:20–21). So some of the apocryphal accounts indicate that all animals recognize him as the Messiah and that he brings the peaceable kingdom to them as well as to humans. In other words, Jesus becomes Savior for the entire creation, other animals included. Still, the critique of the peaceable kingdom imagery, that it takes the "real" animal out of the picture, is one that must be addressed. Can a lion still be a lion if he no longer hunts and eats other animals? Can a hungry wolf feed with lambs, and if so, what will she eat? Still, there is at least a recognition of animals as a worthy part of the creation, a part that Jesus recognizes and that recognizes him.

It is not only wild animals but also domesticated ones working for humans that Jesus encounters in the apocrypha. And certainly, this is not the only place. In the canonical Gospels he reminds listeners that they can break the Sabbath rest to tend to animals: "Does not each of you on the Sabbath untie his ox or his donkey from the manger, and lead it away to give it water?" (Luke 13:15). But this basic compassion for domesticated, laboring animals is expanded in a Coptic apocryphal work, one of the most intriguing accounts of Jesus in relationship with animals. In this story Jesus' empathy extends to a wounded animal:

> It happened that the Lord went forth from the city and walked with his disciples over the mountains. And they came to a mountain, and the road which led to it was steep. There they found a man with a sumpter-mule. But the animal had fallen for the burden was too heavy, and he beat it that it bled. And Jesus came to him and said, Man, why dost thou beat thine animal? Seest thou not that it is too weak for its burden, and knowest thou not that it suffers pains? But the man answered and said, What is that to you? I can beat it as much as I please, since it is my property, and I bought it for a good sum of money. Ask those that are with thee, for they know me and know thereof. And some of the disciples said, Yea Lord, it is as he says. We have seen how he bought it. But the Lord said, Do you notice how it bleeds, and hear you not how it laments and cries? But they answered and said, Nay Lord, we hear not how it laments and cries. And the Lord was sad and exclaimed, Woe to you, that ye hear not how

it complains to the Creator in heaven, and cries for mercy. But three times woe to him of whom it complains and cries in its distress. And he came forth and touched the animal. And it arose and its wounds were healed. And Jesus said to the man, Now go on and beat it no more, that you also may find mercy.[22]

Though the text's origins prove difficult to trace and are, therefore, quite problematic, the story raises challenging alternative perspectives and is thus, in my opinion, worthy of consideration. The disciples, portrayed in ways similar to those in the Gospel of Mark, seem to lack understanding. As a matter of fact, Jesus pronounces "woe" to them because they cannot hear the animal's agony. Jesus also opens up the possibility of an interest in the suffering of animals on the part of God because the donkey cries to the "Creator in heaven" for mercy. God hears, but the disciples and the owner of the donkey do not. In another interesting twist, Jesus connects the owner's lack of compassion for the donkey to his possibility for obtaining mercy! This radical idea suggests that Jesus equates the abuse of an animal with an act that blocks a human from grace. Finally, Jesus counts the donkey worthy of his own healing touch, a tender and powerful moment in the account. Regardless of its apparently untraceable roots, this apocryphal story raises significantly different ways of looking at animals in the varied accounts of Jesus' life.[23]

Elizabeth Schussler Fiorenza wrote a groundbreaking piece, *In Memory of Her: A Feminist Theological Reconstruction of Christian Origins,* in the early 1980s. She proposes that one should not conclude that early Christianity was patriarchal based on the androcentric texts selected for the canon and interpreted by the early church fathers. Rather, "the textual and historical marginalization of women is also a by-product of the 'patristic' selection and canonization process of Scripture."[24] I suggest that the same could be the case with marginalized animals. Of course, sometimes the texts are ones that overlap—those that include women in central roles might also include animals as actors (see the Acts of Paul and Thecla below for a good example of this). Regardless, an ecofeminist reading of the early Christian texts draws on the same reconstructive process defined by Fiorenza. One must critically analyze not only the canonical scriptures but also the process through which some scriptures were selected and others rejected, an androcentric process. This unearths texts that were denied admission into the canon and, in so doing, uncovers the animals present in the extracanonical works.

Animals and Martyrdom in the Apocryphal Acts

The apocryphal acts were composed in the second and third centuries, very early in the Christian tradition. Essentially, they supplement the Acts of the

Apostles in the canonical scriptures, the composition of which remained under debate until the middle of the fourth century.[25] The lives of Andrew, John, Peter, Thomas, and Paul form the major portion of the apocryphal acts, though some female figures, such as Thecla, are also included. These works influenced popular piety by telling stories to uplift newly converted Christians, and, basically, formed the earliest layer of hagiography in the Christian tradition. I focus on the acts here not only because they include animal actors but also because of their apparent popularity. In other words, people heard these stories even when they did not hear the theological treatises beginning to emerge during the same period. It is also true that the apocryphal acts were eventually regarded as heretical by some early Christian leaders. But even Eusebius, who counts many books as "spurious" or "heretical," states that some of the acts, including the Acts of Paul, while "not canonical" are "familiar to most church people."[26]

Themes of martyrdom pervade the Acts because, according to early Christian stories, most of the apostles were executed by state authorities. And because wild animals, often animals who had been captured, abused, and starved, were used in the colosseums throughout the Roman Empire, they intermingle with the stories of martyrs. As mentioned in the previous chapter, animals played the role of attacker when let loose to kill or fight humans in the arena, and attacked when hunted and tortured. Animals died in huge numbers, never receiving the glories of even a few human gladiators. Leonard Thompson describes some of these animals used in the main Colosseum in the city of Rome: "When the Colosseum opened, Titus had 9,000 animals slaughtered in games that included battles between cranes and among four elephants. Lucius Sulla exhibited a combat of 100 maned lions. Augustus sent in 420 female leopards. . . . The greater the number of animals, the more impressive the morning games."[27] As mentioned in the historical outline, "venationes," or staged hunts, were usually held in the Roman arenas in the morning, followed by gladiatorial combats in the afternoon. Thousands, if not hundreds of thousands, of animals, captured at the outskirts of the empire and often considered exotic, died in these staged hunts.

The Acts of Andrew tells a typical story of the encounter between wild beasts, intended by the Roman empire to kill the Christian captives, and potential Christian martyrs. The proconsul in Thessalonica ordered the stadium filled with "beasts" then had Andrew dragged "thither by the hair." But the beasts refused to cooperate: "First they sent in a fierce boar who went about him thrice and did not touch him. The people praised God. A bull led by thirty soldiers and incited by two hunters, did not touch Andrew but tore the hunters to pieces, roared, and fell dead. 'Christ is the true God,' said the people. An angel was seen to descend and strengthen the apostle.

The proconsul in rage sent in a fierce leopard, which left everyone alone but seized and strangled the proconsul's son."[28] In these accounts wild animals refuse to harm Christians while harming those who confront Christianity. God seems to ordain the animals to protect Christians and kill Romans.

One of the most amazing lions appears in the Acts of Paul.[29] An early fragment, in Coptic, tells of a lion approaching Paul as he prayed in a lonely place. The lion lay down at the apostle's feet, and Paul, never missing an opportunity to convert, asked the lion what he wanted. The lion replied, "I want to be baptized." Paul took him to a river and immersed him three times. The lion then greeted Paul with "Grace be with you" and departed into the countryside.[30] Baptism, the Christian sacrament that confirms an active choice of belief and that initiates one into the Christian community, is requested by and granted to a lion.

But this is just the first encounter between the lion and the apostle Paul. Later, as reported in the Acts of Paul and Thecla, on one of his journeys to Ephesus, Paul is captured and "condemned . . . to the beasts." A great display of "beasts" is paraded by the crowds, including one lion who roared "so fiercely and angrily" that "even Paul broke off his prayer in terror." At dawn the next day the spectacle began. The following account tells of the amazing encounter and is quoted at length because of its significance:

> He [Paul] was dragged in, saying nothing but bowed down and groaning be-cause he was led in triumph by the city. And when he was brought out he was immediately flung into the stadium. Everybody was angry at Paul's dignified bearing. . . . So when he had taken his place the [missing text] . . . ordered a very fierce lion which had but recently been captured to be set loose against him. . . . "Away with the sorcerer! Away with the prisoner!" But the lion looked at Paul, and Paul at the lion. Paul recognized that this was the lion which had come and been baptized. And borne along by faith Paul said, "Lion, was it you whom I baptized?" And the lion in answer said to Paul, "Yes." Paul spoke to it again and said, "And how were you captured?" The lion said with its own voice, "Just as you were, Paul." After Hieronymus had sent many beasts so that Paul might be slain, and archers that the lion too might be killed, a violent and exceedingly heavy hail-storm fell from heaven, although the sky was clear: many died and all the rest took to flight. But it did not touch Paul or the lion although the other beasts perished under the weight of the hail. . . . And Paul took leave of the lion, which spoke no more, and went out of the stadium and down to the harbour and embarked on the ship. . . . So he embarked too like one of the fugitives, but the lion went away into the mountains as was natural for it.[31]

This story is rich with animals as symbol and to a certain extent with animals as real animals. First, the parallel stories of Paul and the lion as prisoners because they are both Christian is obvious. The lion was not captured as a beast but was captured "just as" Paul. This leaves the reason for the capture by the authorities open. Was the lion, as a baptized Christian, more susceptible to imprisonment? His "roar" alludes to a difference about him, maybe even to his testimony as a Christian lion. Indeed, his voice is enough to halt Paul in midprayer, something that would certainly be difficult to accomplish. Paul, known as a great preacher, is paralleled by the voice of the lion.

After the mutual recognition between Paul and the lion, the fierce but now obedient Christian feline is also condemned to death by Hieronymus. Does he become a willing martyr at this point, thus displaying the utmost Christian obedience? Beasts enter to kill Paul and archers to kill the lion. Finally, divine intervention saves them both, an honor usually reserved for faithful human martyrs. Although the heavy hailstorm—from heaven of course, as the sky was clear—kills many, it spared not only Paul but also the lion. God spared the baptized—Christian—willing-martyr lion. Quite a few other beasts did die along with some of the human inhabitants of Ephesus, so not all of the animals come out on top here, but the lion was spared.

Certainly the symbolism of the story overwhelms any "real" animal presence. The reality of the lion is not emphasized. But the final departure provides a strange and alluring twist to the story. Paul departs on a boat; the lion went into the mountains. The lion becomes a lion again, speaks no more, and is free. What exactly happened in this series of events between Paul and the baptized lion? Interpretations may vary significantly. But it appears that the lion qua lion exits the scene, saved by his baptism, by his testimony, and by his willingness to accept the martyr's crown. At that point God provides the opportunity for him to be a real, free, and actual lion again, instead of a Christian.

Lions also provide protection for Thecla, a companion of Paul in his journeys. This incident related to her martyrdom shows the connection between Thecla, a female martyr, and the wild animal, a female lion: "And when the beasts were exhibited they bound her to a fierce lioness. . . . And the lioness, with Thecla sitting upon her, licked her feet; and all the multitude was astonished. . . . And Thecla . . . was stripped and received a girdle and was thrown into the arena. And lions and bears were let loose upon her. And a fierce lioness ran up and lay down at her."[32] Indeed, gender, animals, and martyrdom are bound together in the account. A series of animals, some of whom meet their own demise, encounter Thecla during the numerous attempts to execute her. Eventually the lioness dies protecting Thecla. One obvious question, based on Paul's choice to baptize a lion by water, is whether the lioness who dies defending Thecla receives baptism by blood—actual martyr status—in Christianity. Can animals be martyrs, thus achieving the most prestigious form of life and death in Christianity?

Wild animals, however, sometimes do attack potential Christian martyrs. In another popular and interesting story full of gender imagery, the Martydom of Perpetua and Felicitas, the "devil prepared a very fierce cow, provided especially for that purpose contrary to custom, rivaling their sex also in that of the beasts." Rather than befriend the two women, the heifer "tossed" Perpetua and "crushed" Felicitas, though she was not the final cause of their death. Another martyr in this account, Saturus, predicted that he would be killed "by one bite of a leopard." So, when bears were sent out, they did not attack him. Finally, as he predicted, Saturus "with one bite . . . was bathed with such a quantity of blood, that the people shouted out to him as he was returning, the testimony of his second baptism." To a certain extent the animals who kill the martyrs become divine agents too because some early Christians fervently sought and accepted martyrdom. The leopard is, essentially, the agent of the baptism by blood as Saturus is "bathed in his wound."[33] So an early leader of the church, Ignatius of Antioch, arrested by the Romans around 110 CE, eagerly declares, "Let me be food for the beasts through which I can reach God. I am the wheat of God, and I am ground by the teeth of beasts so that I may be found pure bread of Christ. Entice them to become my tomb and leave no trace of my body."[34] Interestingly, while Ignatius longed for the grinding of his flesh, a late Latin record of his martyrdom "tells of the lions that simply lay on him and crushed him so that his body could be preserved intact."[35]

Dogs join lions as prominent figures in the early apocryphal acts. In the Acts of Peter they serve as a mouthpiece for the divine, one actually preaches, and in the Passio dogs recognize Peter and spite Simon Magus, one of Peter's primary rivals. I deal with the text from the Acts of Peter in a later chapter, but a brief look at the Passio provides a glimpse into the role of canines in some of the early apocryphal texts. Peter is in the court of Nero confronting Simon Magus, who had claimed to read the minds of those around him. Peter determines to prove to Nero that Simon is a fraud, and a "contest" ensues. After Peter outwits Simon, the angry magician calls out, "Let great dogs come forth and eat him up before Caesar." Suddenly, three mighty and vicious dogs appear to attack Peter. But Peter had hidden bread up his sleeves, and blessed it, unknown to Simon, though Nero was aware of the hidden loafs. Peter offered the blessed bread to the dogs and the canines "no longer appeared." Though these particular dogs are not messengers of the divine, they certainly recognize the servant of God, Peter, overagainst the enemy of the budding faith, Simon Magus.[36]

As mentioned above, some influential early Christian authorities, such as Jerome and Eusebius, decided not to accept the Acts of Paul, the Acts of Paul and Thecla, or the Acts of Peter as canonical, but the popularity of the works is rarely contested. In direct reference to stories of Paul and lions, Hippolytus, in his *Commentary on Daniel* (written around the year 204 CE), "refers to Paul and the lion without hesitation as orthodox."[37] Metzger continues this line of thought supporting the popularity of the legend in St. Paul and the Baptized Lion: "That this extraordinary tale about the lion was accepted as true by the common Christian layman is shown by the use Hippolytus of Rome made of it early in the third century. In an *argumentum ad hominem* he writes in his *Commentary on Daniel* (iii. 29), 'For if we believe that when Paul was condemned to death, a lion, let loose upon him, fell down and licked his feet, how shall we not believe the things that happened in the case of Daniel?' (in the den of lions)."[38] Even into the late patristic and medieval periods, as Alberto Ferreiro states, the apocryphal writings are "preserved in patristic and medieval homilies, liturgical texts, hagiographies, theological tracts, vernacular literatures, poetry, chronicles, and in art."[39]

So the stories included in texts, though not in the long run deemed worthy for inclusion in the canon, were well known in Christianity. Why? What purpose did they serve? And what might this have to do with the presence of animals in them? Christianity has a literary nature, though for most of its history that meant a literate person reading texts to the many illiterate Christians gathered to hear the stories.[40] The stories in these books served to entertain and to instruct Christians, but when the canon was finally formalized, they did not carry the same weight as the canonical Acts of the Apostles. So a variety of genres naturally appeared and stories were told for different purposes; often the type of text reveals this purpose. Books such as the Acts of Peter seem proto-orthodox, in other words they do support an eventual orthodox position with Peter as the hero and others, such as Simon Magus, as the heretical enemy. Other books, such as the Infancy Gospel of Thomas, seem to emerge when questions were posed about the childhood years of Jesus.

Why, then, do the stories that include animals rarely make their way into the canon? For varying reasons I think. In the case of literature such as the Acts of Paul and Thecla the reason may well be the androcentric bias of the early interpreters who determined the canon. In the case of the Acts of Peter it might be the later date of the text. For the Infancy Gospel of Thomas, certainly the rather problematic images of Jesus as a child who would deliberately harm another child might have contributed. But the androcentric interpretation and selection process is not, in my opinion, the central point in the discussion. Rather, the popularity of the texts, their dissemination across the spectrum of early Christianity, and the widespread acknowledgment of this popularity is more important. Even though the other stories of

Jesus in which he befriends lions and the other stories of the apostles in the presence of preaching dogs do not make the canon, they do enter the popular imagination and become integral to the development of early Christianity.

Animals in Christian Gnosticism

> The superiority of humans is not obvious to the eye but lies in what is hidden. Consequently they have mastery over animals who are stronger and larger in ways apparent and hidden. So the animals survive. When humans withdraw, the animals slay and devour each other, because they do not find food. Now they have food because humans plow the soil. (Gospel of Philip).[41]

In his classic work *The Gnostic Religion,* Hans Jonas describes the beginning of the Christian era as a time of "profound spiritual ferment" focused on a "dualistic transcendent religion of salvation."[42] Although Christianity continues to embody these three traits (dualism, transcendence, and salvation theologies), none of which bode well for other-than-human earthly creatures deemed not to have souls or an afterlife, Gnosticism emphasizes such features even more vigorously. First, it should be noted that Gnosticism is extremely varied with forms emerging over centuries and among different religious traditions. But several strands of early Christian Gnosticism point to the diversity within the religion, even in its infancy.

Gnosis, or knowledge in many complex and mystical forms, is the means of salvation for Gnostic Christianity. This knowledge, within the dualistic transcendent religion of salvation schema suggested by Jonas, leads certain humans, the ones who eventually attain gnosis or have a remnant divine "spark," on a religious quest focused on "ascent to the transcendent realm."[43] While this basic feature is common to most forms of Christianity, Gnosticism adds another element, reinforcing the goal of flight from the material realm. This added element is a distinction between an inferior creator god and a superior transcendent god. Many Gnostic cosmologies describe the created world as a type of mistake or even as an "aborted fetus," a "defect."[44] Then again, the complex mythologies of Gnosticism prove difficult for anybody to unravel. Gnostic truths emerge from myths, not through systematic descriptions; the complexity of these mythologically expressed, hidden truths keeps them covered.

Still, the rather extreme dualism within Gnostic cosmogonies and cosmologies leads to a potentially starker distinction between humans and other animals, indeed, even between different categories of humans, those with the divine spark and those without. Certainly Gnostic texts indicate that all other animals exist for the use of human beings: "Domestic animals may be the bull and the donkey and other species. Others are wild and live in the deserts. A man plows the field with a domestic animal, and from the fruit of his labor he feeds himself and the animals, tame or wild. Compare the perfect human. Through submissive powers he plows and prepares for everything to come into being. So his world holds together, good or evil, the right and the left" (Gospel of Philip).[45] Accordingly, "the superiority of humans is not obvious to the eye but lies in what is hidden. Consequently they have mastery over the animals."[46] In fact, the entire chain of being is laid out in the Gospel of Philip because "the holy spirit" gathers humans and "shuts them in so, like it or not, they cannot escape," just as humans control other animals.[47]

But Gnostic Christianities seem to suggest other possibilities as well. As indicated above, the truths prove difficult to unravel. Within the myriad strands of Gnosticism, another look at the material world, thus at animals, emerges. The Gospel of Thomas, an increasingly well known text, contains several intriguing lines that suggest a kind of wisdom revealed in nature. Although this gospel is not always classified as Gnostic, it does lean toward a gnostic theology.[48] First, the parable of the mustard seed, one of the few triple-attested sayings of Jesus, is included:

> The disciples said to Jesus, "Tell us what the kingdom of heaven is like."
> He said to them, "It is like a mustard seed. It is the smallest of all seeds. But when it falls on tilled soil, it produces a great plant and becomes a shelter for birds of the sky."[49]

Although it might not be the primary point of the parable, the image of a shelter for birds as part of the kingdom of heaven is intriguing. And even more provocative is Jesus self-identification, "It is I who am the all. From me did the all come forth, and unto me did the all extend. Split a piece of wood, and I am there. Lift up the stone, and you will find me there."[50] An initial interpretation of the Gospel of Thomas suggests that animals and other parts of the creation are not excluded from the divine.

The only other life- and body-affirming hints in Gnosticism appear in several of the creation narratives. Gnostics inverted the traditional creation stories of Genesis, making Eve the more prominent of the two human figures. In one case she hides in the tree of life, which becomes a sought-after and allowed provider of wisdom rather than a prohibited bearer of fruit. This creation narrative, in the text On the Origin of the World, also includes the traditional tempter, the "serpent" in Genesis. But here the serpent morphs into the "wisest of creatures" and was even called "Beast."[51] So beasts and serpents, along with trees, find a bit of sacred redemption in Gnostic texts.

Still, an overall picture of Gnostic forms of Christianity does support stark dualisms and hierarchies. Some humans rank above all other humans and the entire material world when issues of salvation, or embodying the divine spark, are concerned. There are few glimpses of hope for animals in these alternative early Christian documents.[52]

Early Christian Theologians and Animals

> But that He should have provided food even for the most savage animals is not a matter of surprise, for these very animals . . . have been created for the purpose of the rational creature.[53] (Origen, third century CE)

Although the complex theological treatises of many early Christian theologians would not have been familiar to the growing population of Christians, the ideas expressed in these treatises filtered into Christian theologies as they continued to develop over the centuries. A brief look at some of the differences, and a suggestion about which school of thought in this ambiguous group of ideas about animals rose to the top, suffices to demonstrate the continued contradictions and tensions within Christianity in its earliest forms.

Origen had no doubt of humanity's superiority to all other animals. Indeed, God ordained this superiority and the rest of creation existed simply for the "purpose" of humanity. As one of the most influential thinkers in the early church, and one whose ideas impacted theologians for generations, his position on animals needs to be examined, at least briefly. The apologetic work *Contra Celsus* contains some of his most straightforward theology regarding the place of animals in the world. Origen lists the beliefs of his opponent regarding the "irrational creatures" then counters each of these. For example, Celsus suggests that humans were created for "other animals" because they hunt humans with weapons "spontaneously provided by nature," whereas humans must create weapons to hunt them. Origen responds with a lengthy list of proofs that animals only exist for humans:

> The creator, then, has constituted all things the servants of the rational being and of his natural understanding. For some purposes we require dogs, say as guardians of our sheep-folds . . . ; and for other purposes we need oxen, as for agriculture; and for others, again, we make use of those which bear the yoke, or beasts of burden. And so it may be said that the race of lions, and bears, and leopards, and wild boars, and such like, has been given to us in order to call into exercise the elements of the manly character that exists within us.[54]

Origen's anthropocentrism knows no bounds; even the primary purpose of wild animals focuses on human use.

One of the lesser known early-fourth-century Christian thinkers is Arnobius of Sicca. A convert from Africa, Arnobius wrote an extended treatise,
Adversus Nationes (Against the Pagans/Heathens). In the midst of this treatise
he introduces the issue of sacrificing to the gods and goddesses. Christian
theology and practice had, essentially, replaced animal sacrifices with the
one-time sacrificial death of Jesus. But in his defense of this Christian position and his attack on "heathen" religious practices of sacrifice, Arnobius
elevates, perhaps unintentionally, the moral status of animals. He suggests
that an ox, or any other animal, would be perfectly justified to approach
the god Jupiter and ask, "Is this, then, O Jupiter, or whatever god thou art,
humane or right, that when another has sinned I should be killed?" The ox
might continue with a more direct criticism of humanity: "Is it because I am
a base creature, and am not possessed of reason and wisdom, as these declare
who call themselves men, and by their ferocity make themselves beasts?" In
other words, humans are the ones endowed with wisdom and thus responsible
for their sins against the divine. But Arnobius's argument goes beyond this
and he equates the very nature of other creatures with that of humanity as
the ox continues his oratory:

> Did not the same nature both beget and form me from the same beginnings?
> Is it not one breath of life which sways both them and me? . . . They love their
> young, and come together to beget children; and do not I both take care to
> procure offspring, and delight in it when it has been begotten? But they have
> reason, and utter articulate sounds; and how do they know whether I do what
> I do for my own reasons, and whether that sound which I give forth is my kind
> of words, and is understood by us alone?

Thus, in the midst of an argument against "heathen" sacrificial practices, Arnobius proceeds to place animals in a position of potential moral equivalence,
or even occasional superiority, to humans. Still, he ends with a basic statement that his entire tirade is for the purpose of discrediting pagan religious
practices, not elevating animals within the creation's hierarchy.[55]

Other positions articulate both the love of God for animals and the superiority of human beings to the other creatures. In his *Divinae Institutiones,*
Lactantius (c. 240–320 CE), an early Christian apologist, student of Arnobius,
and tutor to Constantine's son, describes God as a Creator who cared deeply
about the survival of animals. Although he states that God "did not give that
power of reason to the other animals" that God granted to humans, Lactantius
still believes that God "provided beforehand in what manner their [animal]
life might be made more safe." God protects them from the "severity of frosts
and colds" by clothing them with "their own natural hair." Some animals have

natural weapons, such as "horns" or "hooked talons," whereas others "protect themselves by craft." Of course, according to Lactantius, humans still rise above all the other animals because "the absence of those things which are given to the brutes contributes to the beauty of man."[56]

So early theologians landed on different footings regarding animals and their relationship to both humans and the divine. Although all agreed, in general principle, that animals belong to God's creation and are divinely proclaimed as "good," their purpose in that creation and their status as rational or irrational, moral or immoral (even evil), and utilitarian or worthy in their own right remained debatable.

Conclusions

> Consider the ravens: they neither sow nor reap, they have neither
> storehouse nor barn, and yet God feeds them. Of how much more
> value are you than the birds! (Luke 12:24)

God feeds the ravens and clothes the lilies of the field, but humans are of much more value. This passage from the canonical Gospel of Luke sums up the ambiguity of early Christian texts when other-than-human animals are involved. A dog preaches the word of God yet is still the symbol of the unbaptized ones, unworthy of receiving what is holy. A mule abused by his human owner is healed by Jesus and the owner chastised, even condemned, but still the mule is returned to captivity and labor. A lioness dies protecting Thecla, but nowhere is it clear whether this large feline martyr counts. Does she enter eternal glory and receive baptism by martyrdom as does Thecla? The ambiguities continue throughout the history of Christianity, maybe based on this earliest of patterns. But the stories cannot be told without animals acting as central characters throughout, their voices interjecting a different tale.

It could be argued that the presence of animals serves as a reminder that the Divine related directly to animals as well as humans. So humans cannot claim exclusive access to God; the ontological distance between animals and humans is thus diminished, if not denied altogether. While such an ontological questioning or hierarchical resituating might not be the primary purpose of the apocryphal acts and other early extracanonical texts, it might be an intentional, rather than an unintentional, consequence. The prevalence of animals in these texts in comparison to those included in the New Testament canon is striking. One is simply left wondering why that is the case. Examining the complexities associated with forming the canon are beyond the scope of this study, but the possibilities are definitely intriguing and troubling. Were animals omitted from the canon deliberately as a more dramatic male priesthood, with all of the implications of hierarchy included in that system, is established in the fourth century CE? All of the texts that elevate female figures, such as many of those found in the twentieth century at Nag Hammadi, were left out of the canon. So Mary Magdalene, rather than being a revealer as she is in the Gnostic texts, becomes a prostitute in the tradition of the church. Does the same process happen with other-than-human animals? As the church writes creeds and establishes the nature of Jesus as fully human and fully divine, animals no longer meld with the elevated status of humanity in the cosmic scheme of things. This might be the case.

While the reasons are speculative, the outcomes are explicit. Paul baptized a lion, but lions (except as symbols) no longer participate in the sacraments of the church. But they stubbornly resist the possibility of utter exclusion and continue to gather around those Christians most revered—the saints.

4. Counted among the Saints

Animals in Medieval Hagiography

Saint Anthony, traditionally regarded as the founder of Christian monasticism, thought he was the first monk to live the solitary life until he heard of Paul the Hermit. In the third century CE, Paul left human society and headed for the desert, where he lived in a cave for sixty years. Anthony decided to find the Hermit. As the legend goes, a wolf "came to meet him" and proceeded to lead him to Paul's cave. The Hermit at first refused to speak to Anthony, but finally convinced, the two embraced. Soon, another animal entered the scene: "When it was time for food, a crow flew down, carrying a loaf formed of two halves. Anthony wondered at this, but Paul told him that God provided him daily with food: this day the quantity was doubled to take care of the guest."[1] Somehow the crow knew of Anthony's presence and brought enough food for both of these early Christian saints.

During his time in the wilderness, all of Paul the Hermit's companions had been animals. They knew his location, led the wandering Anthony to him, and provided Paul with nourishment. Paul died shortly after the encounter with Anthony. When Anthony returned and found him dead, he determined to bury him even though he lacked the means. Animals again came to his service. Two lions appeared, "dug a grave, and, when the saint was buried, went back to the forest."[2]

This account is one of the presumably rare appearances of other-than-human animals in the hagiography, edifying stories of saints, of the Christian tradition. But are these animal epiphanies rare or rarely noticed? A careful probing of the stories of the Christian tradition reveals more animals than this religion, often classified as extremely anthropocentric, would seem likely to incorporate. This search for animals and saints seeks to recover a lost strand of silenced animal voices in the history of Christianities.

After studying many written texts and examining numerous visual representations, a framework for understanding the inclusion of animals emerges. Animals appear as saints, as sacraments, as revealers of the divine, as bearers of God or as "imitatio Christi"—imitators of Christ. In these roles animals act, are acted upon, and enact the will of the divine. Amazingly, their agency and power, their action as subjects in their own right, is prominent in myriad stories and is central in numerous images.

The primary sources for these stories are the lives of saints from the third to the sixteenth century CE and religious images throughout the Christian areas of Europe during the same period. Saints, or holy people, are recognized in various religious traditions. For the purposes of this study, I deal with Catholic saints, a fluid category in and of itself, changing over the centuries and shifting along the trajectory between popular religion and institutional religion or authority. The religious imagery on which I focus is popular art, displayed in churches where common people see and interpret its meaning. The hagiographical accounts also served as "liturgical drama," and during the Middle Ages these lives of saints formed part of a public event or ritual cycle.[3] As a result, most Christians, not only the elite, were familiar with the hagiographical accounts. A tracing of these stories and images suggests that certain patterns reveal cultural continuities and shared symbols. The four patterns I address are animals as exemplars of piety, animals as sources of revelation, animals as saintly martyrs, and animals as the primary intimate other in relationship.

In addition, I briefly discuss the phenomenon of the "bestiary." Although bestiaries and the myriad implications for understanding animals are very significant, they are almost totally symbolic and even fantastical, and thus their impact on the lives of real animals is not evident. Certainly, one could argue, all of the stories of animals with saints are potentially and probably symbolic in some way. But the animals themselves are subjects, in some sense, not purely objects. In bestiaries, I argue below, animals are not only imaginary and symbolic but also totally objectified.

In the earliest years of Christianity, martyrs were designated as saints and understood to hold a particular efficacy that assured others the same salvation they attained through their deaths. Over the centuries their shrines, burial places, and feast days served as central devotional sites for Christians. The cult of relics, evidenced by the reliquaries still in existence throughout Europe at the beginning of the twenty-first century, grew rapidly in early Christianity. After the period of state-caused martyrdom ended in the fourth century, certain mystics, monastics, and ascetics filled the ranks of the saints. By the fifth century local bishops had taken "control of the process," and thus we see the growth of "vitas" or lives of saints. Bishops required that a written account of the life of the person considered for sainthood be read aloud in his presence. The body of the saint, if buried already, would be exhumed and moved to an altar, and then a feast day would be assigned.[4] Local calendars of saints developed all over the Christian world through the early Middle Ages.

But in order to secure a "widespread cult," it became increasingly common to seek the authority of the pope regarding who was or was not a saint. This led to a distinction between those who were beatified, or blessed and venerated at a more local level, and those who were canonized, or recognized by the pope as saints and venerated more broadly.[5] Local venerations still included those who were blessed, but only Rome had the authority to formally canonize a saint. Thus, partially in response to the proliferation of saints' designations and shrines, the central authority in Rome intervened, and in 1234 Pope Gregory IX decreed that "only the pope could canonize a saint."[6] Although saints in the modern period are not included in this survey, it should be noted that the process of canonization is rigidly regulated by the Catholic Church, even though John Paul II, one of the longest serving popes in Christian history, saw fit to canonize more saints than all of his predecessors combined.[7]

I return to a note on method here. Although most of the sources are the lives of the saints, another significant component of the research for this chapter included an attempt to see, literally, how widespread some of these stories might be. Various "gaze" theories, then, inform this glimpse into animals in the Christianity of the Middle Ages. Where are their stories seen (in religious imagery) and thus told over and over again? For example, the story of Saint Anthony of Padua and the mule, though problematic because of its anti-Semitic theme, is also one that was widespread, as evidenced by the images depicting this story. Looking at the story again, with a feminist gaze, might mean something as basic as suggesting the opening of the Eucharist to other-than-human beings. If an image of a mule kneeling before the host gazes at those gathered in the baptistery in Siena, might that not suggest that a real mule can partake? Or if the reciprocity between saints and the animals that inhabit the wilderness with them is embedded through story and image, can such a real relationship of reciprocity emerge? The lens of interpretation of these prevalent stories, and a rethinking of them from a different perspective, could lead to a radical reformation of the relationship between humans and animals in traditional Christianity.

Animals as Exemplars of Piety

> At their approach to the harbor of this island, all the birds began to
> sing, as if saying with one voice: "Victory to our God who sits upon
> the throne and to the Lamb" (Rv 7:10). And again: "The Lord God
> has shone upon us. Bind the sacrifice with cords, as far as the horns
> of the altar" (Ps 117:27). They sang with their voices and flapped
> with their wings for almost half an hour.[8]

Amazingly, birds quote Scripture with their voices and their wings. *The Voyage of Brendan,* a tenth-century Irish text, tells the story of a saint who traveled widely and encountered numerous animals in his journeys. Of course, this hagiography, like many others, combines various traditions and tales, but the presence of "Christianized" animals throughout is fascinating. While the monks traveling the waters with Brendan fear the animals in the sea and ask the saint to "celebrate Mass silently in case the creatures should hear them and rise up to attack them," Brendan understands the animals and brings them into the Christian community. He responds to his brothers, "Surely our Lord Jesus Christ is God of all these creatures, and can subdue them all?" It seems, however, that subduing them is not necessary. Brendan begins Mass "at the top of his voice" while the brothers watch with anxiety. The creatures, when they "heard his voice, rose up from the seabed and began to swim around the boat so that these same creatures were all the monks could see about them. They did not approach the boat but swam to and fro some distance away until the man of God had completed his Mass. Then all the creatures vanished from sight, turning tail in all directions along the many paths of the sea."[9] Rather than attack the monks, the creatures, basically, attended Mass then headed on their way back to sea.

Similar incidents abound in hagiographical accounts. As mentioned earlier, the first generation leader of the church, Paul, met and baptized a lion who later spared the apostle in a Roman circus. As I suggest in the study of the early extracanonical acts, particularly those related to human martyrs, other animals, arguably, filled the sacrament of baptism by blood when they were martyred along with early Christians. But in addition to the sacraments of baptism (by water and by fire), do animals participate in any of the other sacraments?

Apparently, animals have been invited to partake in the ritual of the Eucharist as well. In Donatello's portrayal (*The Miracle of the Mule,* bronze, Basilica del Santo, Padua, Italy), the scene is the celebration of the Eucharist, the central act of many forms of Christian worship, and of a mule kneeling before the host, the body and blood of Christ.[10] This ultimate liturgical moment in most Christian worship rituals, this sacrament, is most fully adored by a mule. Saint Anthony, often dubbed the greatest preacher of his time, is a young Franciscan who preaches to fish much as his predecessor, Saint Francis, preached to the birds. The miracle of the mule suggests the incorporation of animals into both the liturgy and the sacramental life of the church. The image appears in highly acclaimed works of art, such a Donatello's, and on the walls of baptisteries frequented by the most common of people.[11]

A parallel pattern is revealed throughout the stories of the life of St. Francis of Assisi. Myriad animals relate with Francis, and many artistic renderings of his life include birds, wolves, and donkeys in company with the saint. Even images of Francis in ecstasy, at the height of mystical union with the divine, include animals.

But a particularly poignant tale reveals the piety of the birds:

> As St. Francis spoke these words to them, all those birds began to open their beaks, and to stretch out their necks, and to open their wings, and reverently to bow their heads to the ground, and to show by their motions and by their songs that the holy father had given them very great delight. St. Francis rejoiced with them and was glad and marveled much at so great a multitude of birds and at their most beautiful diversity, and at their attentiveness and fearlessness, for which he devoutly praised the Creator in them.[12]

An "infinite multitude" of birds, Francis addresses them as "little sisters," gather and attentively listen to Francis as he preaches about their blessedness and their need to praise God.

According to two of Francis's biographers, he "blessed them, and having made the sign of the cross, gave them leave to fly away to another place. . . . [N]or did one of them move from the spot until he made the sign of the cross over them and give them leave." Upon leaving, another symbol of piety emerges, as "all those birds soared up into the air with wondrous songs and then divided themselves into four parts after the form of the cross Saint Francis had made over them."[13] The birds then proceed to announce their own belief:

> One band flew toward the East, and one toward the West, and one toward the South and the fourth toward the North, and each company went singing marvelous songs. Thus they signified that, just as St. Francis, the Standard-bearer of the Cross, had preached to them, and made over them the sign of the Cross, according to which they separated themselves toward the four quarters of the world, so the preaching of the Cross of Christ, renewed by St. Francis, was about to be carried through all the world by him and by his friars. Moreover, these friars, like the birds, possess nothing of their own in this world but commit their lives wholly to the providence of God.[14]

Of course, the Christian imperialistic implications and difficulties of this passage are apparent, but the amazing indication of birds as committing their lives to God shifts anthropocentric paradigms significantly. St. Francis was neither the first nor the last to recognize that birds and other creatures comprise a congregation worthy of preaching. They not only hear the word but also are capable of response to it. This active response to the word of God is an important concept in Christianity. The birds are infinitely capable of worship and, apparently, of belief in God.

St. Francis Preaching to the Birds by Gozzoli, Montefalco, Italy. Photo taken by author; courtesy of Museo Civico di San Francesco, Montefalco.

Another animal whose piety testifies to those around is a cricket. Francis, having risen before the sun for prayer, finds that the world is blanketed in snow. None of the other brothers comes to early morning prayers because of the cold. But a cricket braves the snow, leaving a trail, and joins Francis for prayer. When the other brothers finally awake, they see the cricket footprints and find the two—Francis and the pious cricket—attending to their sacred office.

One of the primary scenes attesting to animals as exemplars of piety is also one of the most powerful symbolic-visual sets of images in Christian history—stories of the nativity of Jesus. These stories include images of adoring animals surrounding the manger. Cattle, sheep, donkeys, and the occasional dog or horse prove uncanny in their ability to recognize the revelation of incarnation of the nativity. Indeed, some images depict humans as much less aware of the nature of the incarnation than were the animals. Images carved in marble, ivory, and stone from the earliest generations of Christianity show the donkey and the cow nuzzling the baby Jesus. In one of these, the donkey is obviously kissing him. Other portrayals depict all of the humans in the scene turned away from the infant, but the cow and donkey still gaze at him attentively, often smiling. The animals' affinity for the sacred is obvious, and their incorporation into scenes of piety is dramatic.

Animals as Sources of Revelation

Animals have also been direct sources of revelation—messengers of the divine to human beings. In particular, animals have been the bearers or carriers of the incarnation of the sacred—the bearers of Christ.

While hunting one day, a Roman soldier, Placidus, came upon a herd of deer. One of these, a large stag, impressed the soldier with his incredible size and beauty. As the stag ran into the dense woods, the soldier followed, pondering how to capture this animal. Suddenly he noticed a cross with the image of Jesus between the antlers of the deer. The voice of the divine came from the stag's mouth and said, "O Placidus, why are you pursuing me? For your sake I have appeared to you in this animal. I am the Christ, whom you worship without knowing it. Your alms have risen before me, and for this purpose I have come, that through this deer which you hunted, I myself might hunt you."[15] The next morning, the vision appeared to him, again with the stag as the vehicle for revelation. The soldier changes his name to Eustace and becomes Christian. His tale relates yet another animal saint. Years later, when Eustace was placed in the arena for martyrdom, a ferocious and very hungry lion served as the imperial death weapon of choice. But the lion came out peacefully, lowered his head, and adored the soon-to-be martyrs rather than kill them.

A similar story is told of Saint Julian, who had "unwittingly" killed his parents. "When this Julian, noble by birth, was young, he went out one day to hunt and began to chase a stag whose trail he had picked up. Suddenly, by the will of God, the stag turned to face him and said: 'Are you tracking me to kill me, you who are going to kill your father and mother?' Filled with dread at hearing this, and fearing that what he had heard from the stag might indeed happen to him, he left everything and went away secretly." Needless to say, the young man did, accidentally, kill his parents. But this horrid act led him to establish a hospice in order to work out his penance. He and his wife spent their lives "full of good works and almsgiving."[16]

St. Francis Xavier tells of a related vision of the divine. During a mighty storm in the Moluccas, Xavier tried to calm the waves by holding his crucifix over them, but a huge wave swept it overboard. Once safely on shore, Francis saw a large crab coming towards him, carrying the cross in his pincers—the bearer of the most sacred symbol of the divine.[17]

Although these stories tell more direct encounters with the divine through an animal, a legend connected with Simeon Stylites portrays an animal in a somewhat more complicated role. Simeon, the ultimate example of Syrian asceticism, probably lived in the fifth century. Several accounts of his life survive. From these we know that he was widely respected as a wise judge and miracle worker. People traveled from great distances on pilgrimage to witness his ascetic, faithful life (he lived a portion of his life on top of a tall pillar) and to merely be in his presence. Worms are particularly prevalent in stories about Simeon, but one story regarding another animal, from Antonius's life of Simeon, stands out:

> Hear another strange and extraordinary mystery. Some people were coming from far away to have him pray [for them] when they came across a pregnant hind grazing. One of them said to the hind, "I adjure you by the power of the devout Simeon, stand still so that I can catch you." Immediately the hind stood still; he caught it and slaughtered it and they ate its flesh. The skin was left over. Immediately they could not speak to one another, but began to bleat like dumb animals. They ran and fell down in front of [the saint's] pillar, praying to be healed. The skin of the hind was filled with chaff, and placed on display long enough for many men to know about it. The men spent sufficient time in penance and, when they were healed, returned home.[18]

Interpretations for this obviously pedagogical story vary. On the one hand, the hind seems to be the most faithful actor in the drama because she stands still based on the invocation of Simeon's name. And because her obedience leads to her death, she could be interpreted as a martyr or at least martyrlike. But are the people who kill her called to repent for killing the hind or are they called to repent for invoking the name of Simeon to do so? That is a more difficult and nuanced interpretation of the story. Indeed the hind becomes a teaching tool while held on display, but the hearer of the story must determine the lesson.

In more general visual presentation, the image of the donkey, already a focus in the nativity images addressed above, is central again. The donkey, referred to as the bearer of the salvation of the world, carries Mary, the mother of Jesus, when she is pregnant and traveling to Bethlehem. Next, the donkey carries Mary and Jesus to safety in Egypt when the infant is being pursued by Herod the Great. Various images show Mary and Joseph feeding the donkey and gazing at him attentively.[19] Finally, the donkey bears Jesus on his back during the triumphant entry into Jerusalem before Jesus' execution. The depiction of this scene is one of the most prominent in early Christianity. It could be argued that Christianity, as a whole, elevated the status of the ass. When others mock Jesus or fail to notice the signs of revelation, the donkey comes through—adoring, worshiping, and carrying the incarnate God.

Animals as Martyrs and Servants

The most striking images of animals in the hagiography are those of animals as martyrs and animals as servants. The martyr, or witness, was and is elevated as the most faithful of all Christians. Following the example set by Jesus, martyrs claimed a second and ultimate baptism in blood. Their stories were told throughout Christianity to strengthen the commitments of believers facing oppression. But some of these martyrs are not just symbolically but literally sacrificial lambs.

The complex stories about dogs as martyrs are addressed in another chapter because canines are so prevalent in the hagiographical accounts and in Christian histories as a whole. Certainly, the myriad martyrdom stories, such as those connected to Guinefort, need to be recalled here.[20]

In the year 406, Paulinus, a monk and a priest, read a poem honoring St. Felix on his birthday. The poem features animals as the principal characters in a series of miracle tales. Christianity had denounced animal sacrifice, primarily as a mode of differentiation from Roman religious systems. But the ritual continued, particularly in rural areas. At the tomb of St. Felix, in southern Italy, the practice had been Christianized and served as a way to distribute food to the poor who would gather at the tomb to collect meat from the sacrificed animals.

The first tale is of a horse "seemingly endowed with human reason" who provided a "holy sign" and became a "source of wonder for those in attendance."[21] This inspired horse intervened as his master attempted to take the best portions of a hog that he had sacrificed rather than leave them for the poor. The horse threw the greedy one to the ground, and then this equine saint carried the sacrifice back to the tomb. Power and compassion are central to this horse-saint's piety.

A second story comes from this same tradition and relates the miracle of a rather plump pig. She had been vowed to Felix at birth, but because of her girth she was unable to walk the distance to the shrine. Her masters decided to take two smaller piglets in her place, but when they arrived, the pudgy pig was on the altar offering herself as sacrifice. Obviously, the sacred had been revealed in and through the pig, who by some accounts placed her throat on the blade, willingly offering her life as food that others might live. A similar story tells of a heifer who walks without a harness to the altar. Then, "undefiled by the yoke and offering its neck to the axe, about to provide food for the poor from its slaughtered body, joyously it poured out its blood in fulfillment of its masters' vows."[22] Parallels between the sacrificial role of these animals and that of the figure of Jesus, particularly in their theological connotations, are both striking and controversial.

Of course, the lamb is a pervasive visual and liturgical symbol of sacrifice and piety, oftentimes replacing the figure of Jesus and other disciples. A beautiful example of such an image is in the seventh-century apse of Sant' Apollinare in Classe, Italy, which portrays all of the twelve traditional disciples as sheep.[23] So the symbol of animals as sacrificial victims and even as savior is central to Christianity. But the stories of St. Felix move these animals into active roles, symbolic and actual in their life of sacrifice.

Another common theme of animals as servants comes at the time of death and burial. Lions are often central to these stories, abounding in Christian legend and symbol. For centuries lions stood on either side of many bishop's seats in cathedrals and framed the doors of many churches, including the church in which the young St. Francis was baptized—San Ruffino in Assisi, Italy. Of course, lions had been a dominant religious symbol before the emergence of Christianity as well.[24]

A story similar to that of Saints Paul and Anthony tells of another lion assisting in the burial of a saint. St. Mary of Egypt, a hermit and ascetic, had lived in the desert for years, eating only the lentils and meager supply of bread to which she had access. A monk, Zosimus, came across this figure of holiness as he traversed the desert. One year he served her the Eucharist and promised to bring this sacrament to her the next year as well. When he came back, he found her dead: "Zosimus tried to dig a grave but could not. Then he saw a lion meekly coming toward him and said to the lion: 'This holy woman commanded me to bury her body here, but I am old and cannot dig, and anyway I have no shovel. Therefore you do the digging and we will be able to bury this holy body.' The lion began to dig and prepared a suitable grave, and when that was finished went away like a gentle lamb."[25] With care and tenderness, the lion dug a perfect hole for St. Mary, the ground was blessed, and she was buried there.

The theme of holy people in the wilderness being tended to by animals continues in the traditions of one of the desert fathers, Abba Macarius. While returning from a pilgrimage the Abba's bread and water gave out, leaving him in a "very precarious position." God intervened through a herd of antelope:

> [I]mmediately the antelope turned over and [showed] me her breasts streaming with milk. Then I knew right away that God wished to keep me alive and I heard a voice, "Macarius, arise, go to the antelope, drink the milk, and recover your strength and go to your cell." He went and drank her milk and slept a little. The antelope went away and one of them, either her or another one, gave him milk each day. "And when I drew near my cell and was a day's walk from it, all the antelope went away and left me. I returned to my cell on the eighth day."[26]

Animals, even arachnids, seem to hear the voice of God. Another story connected to a saint named Felix includes spiders as heroes. While preaching, Felix, a bishop, found himself being pursued by persecutors, so he proceeded to hide. He "slipped through a narrow opening in the wall of a ruined house and hid there. In a trice, by God's command, spiders spun a web across the space. The pursuers, seeing the web, thought that no one could have gone through the opening, and went on their way."[27] Later Felix was killed by a group of boys he taught. Apparently they were less compassionate than the spiders.

Animals as "Primary Other" in Relationship

Finally, there are numerous stories throughout the Christian tradition of animals as the primary other in relationship to humans. Obviously many of the hermits and desert dwellers mentioned throughout are in the company of an animal or animals. In addition, anchoresses who lived cloistered lives, often as solitaries, would be permitted one cat in their cell, as iconography connected to Julian of Norwich suggests. But one of the most popular stories of saint-animal companionship is that of St. Jerome, a father of the church.

St. Jerome lived in the wilderness, probably close to Bethlehem, while translating the Bible from Greek into Latin. He lived with some other monks, and many animals, including dogs, hens, sheep, and donkeys. On an otherwise normal day, a great lion came into the monastery courtyard. Needless to say, all the monks scattered, except for Jerome. He noticed that the lion was limping and welcomed him in the spirit of hospitality that pervades most monasteries. Jerome healed the lion, who decided to remain with Jerome. The adventures of Jerome and the lion continue, but suffice it to say that on the death of the saint, the lion, a saint in his own right, is said to have grieved without ceasing.

This is not the only such account. The story of St. Giles and the hind is tender and tragic. Giles, who had cured many, became a solitary living in a cave close to a beautiful spring. But he was only a solitary in terms of his relationship with people, because as the story goes, "for some time he was nourished with the milk of a hind" or doe. Eventually, a group of hunters pursued her, and she took refuge with St. Giles in his cave. She was "whining and whimpering . . . not at all like her," so Giles went out and, hearing the

St. Jerome and the Lion by Gozzoli, Montefalco, Italy. Photo taken by author; courtesy of Museo Civico di San Francesco, Montefalco

hunt, prayed that God would save this doe, the "nurse" God had provided. This happened again and again, until finally, on the third day, the king brought a bishop along with him to survey the situation. This time "one of the huntsmen shot an arrow into the cave," wounding St. Giles as he knelt in prayer for the life of the doe.[28]

St. Blaise, a bishop, also decided to live the life of a hermit. He "retired to a cave" where "birds brought him food, and wild animals flocked to him." These animals would not leave "until he had laid hands on them in blessing," an action that indicates Blaise understood the animals worthy of blessing and the animals understood the significance of the ritual. In addition, Blaise offered them healing, and "if any of them were ailing, they came straight to him and went away cured."[29]

In *The Voyage of Brendan,* the monks come to an island inhabited by a hermit, aptly named Paul. The hermit relates his own story to the gathered monks. After he had lived in the monastery of St. Patrick for years, God instructed him to go to the shore and climb into a boat. After sailing for three days and three nights, he landed on the island: "And I remained here. At about three o'clock in the afternoon a sea otter would bring me food from the sea walking on its hind legs, carrying a fish in its jaws and with a bundle of twigs for making a fire between its legs. When it had placed before me the fish and the twigs, it returned to the sea. I lit a fire with flint and iron and prepared a meal from the fish. This continued for thirty years with the otter bringing me food, a fish, every three days."[30] God sustained Paul for three decades through a relationship with an otter.

But the primary other certainly extends in both directions in these relationships. Animals provide companionship for saints such as Paul and Jerome, but saints also deem animals worthy of their healing and protective powers, as exemplified so powerfully by St. Giles. Macarius is another early saint who tends to the emotional and physical lives of the animals in his desert world. Here, in a powerful story about baby goats, the saint becomes symbol of God's compassion for the entire creation:

> One time when I was in the wadi gathering palm branches, an antelope came up to me, tearing out its fur, weeping as though it were a he-goat, its tears flowing to the ground. It threw itself down on top of my feet and moistened them with its tears, and I sat down and stroked its face and anointed it with my hands, amazed at its tears, while it gazed back at me. After a while it took hold of my tunic and pulled on me. I followed it through the power of our Lord Jesus Christ and when it took me to where it lived, I found its three young lying there. When I sat down, it took hold of them one by one and placed them in my lap and when I touched them I found that they were deformed: their chins

were on their backs. I took pity on them as their mother wept; I groaned over them, saying, "You who care for all of creation, our Lord Jesus Christ, who have numerous treasuries of mercy, take pity on the creature you made." After I said these words accompanied by tears before my Lord Jesus Christ, I stretched out my hand and made the saving sign of the cross over the antelope's young, and they were healed.

At that point Macarius returned the healed babies to their mother, who "rejoiced over them, delighting in them." The saint proceeds to marvel at the goodness of God and, especially, for "the multitude of his mercies for every creature he has made."[31] Other, similar stories of healing, companionship, compassion, and peaceful coexistence abound in the lives of the desert ascetics.

The Count de Montalembert (1819–1870) contributed a six-volume work on the lives of monks, from St. Benedict to St. Bernard, in the late nineteenth century. Although he draws on many earlier works for these hagiographical accounts, it is interesting to consider his interpretation of the relationships between monks and "wild" animals. Montalembert says that the ancient authors who report on the devotion of animals to saints "are unanimous in asserting that this supernatural empire of the old monks over the animal creation is explained by the primitive innocence which these heroes of penitence and purity had won back, and which placed them once more on a level with Adam and Eve in the terrestrial Paradise."[32] This of course raises the question of whether saints possessed the ability to reestablish the prelapsarian world of innocent relationship with other species or to reembed the dominance over nature imaged in the Adam of Genesis 2, who wields the power of naming animals. Montalembert leans toward the second interpretation, suggesting that a "miracle" restored to "man" through the monks "the empire and use of creatures which God had given him for instruments." Animals had "relapsed into a savage condition," and these early monk-saints succeeded in a "civilizing mission," even among other-than-human creatures.[33]

Bestiaries

Alan of Lille (1125–1203), a theologian who spent much of his life fighting the Catharist heresy, placed animals in the midst of the symbolic order: "Omnis mundi creature Quasi liber et pictura Nobis est et speculum." (Every creature of the world is as a book or picture, and also a mirror for us.)[34] The tradition of the bestiary—medieval animal illustrations found in books, engraved in churches, and even used in sermons—involved connecting certain physical or behavioral qualities or traits with the divine plan. Basically, bestiaries are catalogues with images and descriptions of various animals, some real and others fantastic (such as the unicorn). This animal catalog, based on the Greek *Physiologus,* assigns certain moral and spiritual lessons to each of the animals described. As imaged and told in bestiaries, the book of nature revealed God's scheme and animals often embodied, literally, the divine purpose. They functioned pedagogically with text and image reinforcing Christian doctrine and morality. Of course, this allegorical concept was not a new one, and in addition to the *Physiologus,* it is reflected in various ancient texts, such as the book of Proverbs.[35]

Dorothy Yamamoto offers a positive interpretation of bestiaries, at least positive in the sense that animals reveal primarily the good order of creation and do, at times, disclose moral virtues to humans. Though animals "do not choose to act the way they do," the "bodily identity of each creature" reveals the divine blueprint.[36] So she describes the bestiary images of fish, who "maintain bonds with each other of absolute purity and fidelity . . . never, ever, guilty of adultery with strange fish" and of the "hoopoe" that "cares for its parents when they grow old, preening their feathers, keeping them warm, and cleaning their eyes."[37] In the long run, however, Yamamoto does conclude that bestiaries remain firmly within a Thomistic hierarchical scheme and rarely allow the observer to stray from the status quo.

In her essay on animals in medieval bestiaries, Beverly Kienzle suggests that Augustine of Hippo's theory of signification had an impact on medieval exegetes' interpretation of animals. Animals become "objects . . . theoretically excluded from communion with humans."[38] They have didactic value, but no other real purpose. However, by the twelfth century, when heresies were wild and growing throughout Europe (particularly the southern areas), bestiaries, mirroring that growth, started to reveal more animals symbolized as heretics. So although many saints lived in companionship with animals, those creating some of the most dominant visual images portrayed animals, or pseudo-animals, in relationship to heretics and the devil. Kienzle lists several animals that become prime types for heretics: wolves, foxes, cats, dogs, fallow deer, leopards, jackals, and moths.

Even though bestiaries dealt with symbolic animals, their impact must be acknowledged. From the twelfth to the fifteenth century, vernacular versions of the Latin manuscripts circulated widely in Europe. As Florence McCulloch pointed out in her seminal study, illustrations were particularly prevalent in the vernacular versions.[39] And as pointed out by Clark and McMunn, the dissemination of these texts was probably the result of the use of "beast-moral literature as an instructional tool for those who were not functionally literate."[40] They served a didactic purpose, as did the hagiographies. In both cases, then, animals figured prominently, though for different reasons.

Conclusions

With bestiaries and saints in mind, where did animals stand in relationship to humans during this long time period, the so interestingly named "Middle Ages"? Their position is not well defined. A glimpse at a most storied animal, the wolf, helps open the tension for animals as subjects or objects, as us or as them.

One of the most popular legends of Francis of Assisi is his encounter with the wolf of Gubbio. A "great wolf, terrible and fierce . . . devoured animals but also men and women" in the small town of Gubbio, not far from Assisi. Francis, in his compassion, approached the wolf, who "lunged at St. Francis with open jaws." The saint made the sign of the cross and commanded the wolf to "come hither . . . do no harm to me or to any other." Then a miracle occured, and the wolf, "gentle as a lamb," laid himself at the feet of Francis. The saint then spoke to "friar wolf," asking him to make peace with the people of the city and telling the wolf that in return, he would ask that the human residents of Gubbio feed the wolf regularly so he would never be hungry again. Then, in a scene depicted in images all over Italy, the saint and the wolf went in front of all of the people and vowed to keep their pledge. The "wolf, lifting up his right paw, put it in the hand of St. Francis." The wolf lived among the people of the town for two years, entering "familiarly into its houses, going from door to door, neither doing injury to anyone nor receiving any." They nourished him until, "after two years, friar wolf died of old age, at which the citizens lamented much."[41] Was this a real wolf? As with the other stories of animals and saints, that question is important, but maybe less important than the overall idea of human and wolf in communion with each other. Also, the possibility of this encounter being one that is true, or at least true in the sense of the life of St. Francis, remains.

Wolves in bestiaries, though, fare much worse. The wolf is "rabid and rapacious"; it "destroys all in its path."[42] Certainly the wolf of Gubbio was doing the same, but Francis entered into a relationship with him. Bestiaries exclude the possibility of such relationship with other species. In bestiaries, and in numerous other pieces of literature, the wolf always represents the devil and is a primary symbol of evil. Not only in bestiaries but also in more formal theological treatises the wolf symbolizes evil. Hildegard of Bingen's major treatise, *Scivias,* lists "five ferocious epochs of temporal rule," each

Wolf, folio 16 v., Aberdeen bestiary. Photo courtesy of the University of Aberdeen, King's College, Scotland.

represented by an animal: the fiery dog, the yellow lion, the pale horse, and the black pig. The "gray wolf" is the last, symbolizing those who "plunder each other."[43]

The "animal other" has no agency and cannot be like the human in its choice of character or way of being. In the bestiary, animal is other, is object, is ordained for humanity. The gaze of the bestiary is one focused solely on human beings. While animals are present, they are symbol and object without agency. In many ways, this is the role assigned to animals in the Middle Ages. But from other perspectives, from the lives of some of the saints, a different gaze or position is assumed and animals are subjects with some agency.

So can animals be counted among the saints in Christianity? They served as the locus for revelation, as exemplars of piety, as martyrs and servants, and, in their relationships with others, they have been the source of agape—the love of the divine. Thus the sacred history, though often obscured, suggests that animals may indeed be counted among the holy ones in the Christian tradition. Of course, the functional worldview for these animal-human-divine relationships reveals a significantly different historical context in many cases. Humans and animals were intimately related in everyday life at the time these stories were developed. In contrast, Euro-American culture of the early twenty-first century is a culture alienated from the natural world and other animals in most manifestations. Popular images of animals have morphed into human projections on a vast scale—from *The Lion King* to cultlike pedigree dog shows to mass-produced flesh for food, with the actual dead animal being an utterly absent referent. These differences could, arguably, render the relevance of such animal stories impotent.

Still, the stories of animals with saints obviously do not tell the entire story. Bestiaries and the hierarchical cosmology of dominant, anthropocentric theological constructs reveal another cultural perspective from the same time period. Animals seem always contested, in both communion and contrast.

But even in those different cultural contexts saints provided an alternative relationship. Andrew Linzey, one of the few contemporary theologians to address the issue of animals, suggests this possibility in his book *Animal Theology*: "We need to remember that the challenge of so many saints in their love and concern for even the most hated of all animals, was in almost all cases *against* the spirit of their times. Christian authorities have been forgetful or indifferent to the claims of animals, or perhaps more accurately, simply misled by *ad hoc* theological speculations."[44] Such subversive stories of liberation for animals were required throughout the first sixteen centuries of Christianity. Interestingly, these stories of animals are connected to the stories of the most pious, the holiest of all—the saints.

I suggest that retelling stories of animals as saints could evoke radical attempts at reconstructing Christianity and could help to promote critical reflection on human-animal relationships. In her introduction to a volume of women's writings in American religion, Rosemary Skinner Keller states that "until history is revised, neither the writer nor the readers can imagine how a different story of the tradition will change their lives or the shape of history itself. When history is revised, the writer and the reader are led to new beginning points for interpreting their heritages. Neither person can accept the old story as it was told before!"[45]

5. The Granted Image

Dogs in Christian Story and Art

In the movie *Michael*, a story of the archangel who has come to visit Earth for the last time, one of the main characters is a little terrier named Sparky.[1] Sparky's role is central to the story in many ways: he's the darling of the tabloid reporting on the archangel, he causes the female lead to enter the drama, and the movie's climactic scene involves his resurrection. Sparky proves to be a handful for everyone except Huey, his primary trainer, and the Archangel Michael. When Sparky runs out in front of an oncoming eighteen-wheeler, we know that the huge truck will hit and kill him, and it does. But then Michael, played by John Travolta, scoops his dead, limp body into his angel arms and resurrects the little dog. It's a touching scene as Michael wraps his feathered wings around the terrier then infuses him with life and energy. The devastated people who witnessed the dog's death weep with joy when Sparky returns to life. But because of the power expended in this resurrection, Michael's feathers drop even more rapidly from his wings, his angelic powers used up by his compassion for Sparky (and for the humans begging the angel to bring Sparky back to life). The movie features other brief encounters with animals. For example, Michael engages in a head-butting contest with a large bull in one of the earliest scenes, apparently reminiscent of similar competitions the angel engaged in throughout his thousands of years of existence. But what is it about dogs? Why does Sparky become the catalyst for the drama?

Research on the origin of the human-canine relationship suggests that the two species have lived together for at least fifteen thousand years, though some recent, and highly controversial, interpretations of DNA evidence push that date back to over one hundred thousand years.[2] So humans and dogs have cohabitated for generations, in various forms of relationship. Herding dogs, search and rescue dogs, service dogs, show dogs, companions (pets), and those dogs who are hardly ever noticed, just part of the background of other events, live in the midst of humans and humans live in the midst of them. And certainly, there are numerous dogs, as there are numerous people, who have no socially acceptable place in modern culture. But as a whole, dogs and humans have evolved in relationship together for at least 150 centuries, and probably longer than that, maybe from the emergence of *Homo sapiens* as a species. One would be remiss to study human history without even mentioning canines as a part of the story.[3]

How and why did this interspecies relationship come about? Some theories point toward artificial selection; humans picked certain relatively tame wolves and, over generations, bred them into domesticated wolves, from *Canis lupus* to *Canis familiaris*. A feminist twist enters this dialogue with the suggestion of "women as early domesticators of the dog."[4] Theories based around such human-dominated artificial selection lost support as alternative theories indicated that wolves took at least some of the initiative in forming this interspecies bond when "wolf wannabe dogs" took "advantage of the calorie bonanzas provided by humans' waste dumps."[5] Certain wolves were, and are, less likely to flee from humans than others. Some of these same wolves, usually not the dominant ones, needed to find alternative sources for food if they found themselves at the bottom of the pack hierarchy. At the varying points in human history when more permanent communities were established, humans also began accumulating waste in close proximity to these settlements. The wolves who did not flee and who needed food scavenged from these trash dumps. Eventually, through a process of modified natural selection, they became domesticated dogs or, as Raymond and Lorna Coppinger call them, "village dogs."[6] Myriad examples of village dogs still exist throughout the world.[7]

Compelling and controversial theories, such as the interpretations of DNA mentioned above, constantly emerge from various research fields (biology, anthropology, animal behavior/ethology, archaeology, and others).[8] John Allman, an evolutionary biologist, proposes that the partnership between humans and dogs led to the success of humans over other hominid species such as *Homo erectus* and Neanderthals. He suggests that our ancestors migrated out of Africa and into Europe with dogs, thus benefiting them with the canine hunting capacity and allowing *Homo sapiens* to continue migrating into inhospitable areas, such as the Arctic Circle. Because both wolves (and dogs) and humans live in extended family situations, the two species were well suited to live together.[9]

Certainly, both species benefited each other in various ways. Domesticated dogs eventually helped hunter-gatherers with their hunting tasks. They also began guarding functions early in the partnership. More specialized canine functions, such as herding and retrieving, developed later in the process of coevolution and point to a significant, complex, and mature level of human intervention in both breeding and behavior. Because of the ascendancy of *Homo sapiens* as a power species on the planet, dogs, in this association with humans, benefited in their sheer evolutionary success. There are four hundred million dogs in the world, a thousand times more dogs than wolves.[10] Some researchers suggest that the earliest would-be dogs made a type of evolutionary decision, though a subconscious or unconscious one, to link themselves to humans. If that is the case, the decision has served *Canis familiaris* and *Homo sapiens* well.

Therefore it seems that some wolves selected cohabitation with humans and some humans accepted wolves so that, over generations, these canines evolved into the domestic dog. Did humans survive as a species because of this relationship? Did dogs "hunt" humans through the Ice Age that brought Neanderthals to an end? Did canines functioning as the primary "smellers" allow the human face to be freed up for oral communication? In other words, are we such talkers because dogs became the smellers for us? Compelling theories abound. Many are particularly enticing for dog lovers worldwide. All of these assertions will remain theoretical and can be interpreted variously depending on one's particular position or agenda, as is the case with theories in any discipline or area of research.

Regardless of one's place in this ongoing dialogue, though, the dog-human relationship offers a fascinating story and the only one of its kind in human–other species connections. Scholars across many disciplines recognize this unique history. For example, increasing numbers of archaeologists note that "the dog is literally the only animal that prehistorians around the world have in common"; thus the "history of the dog" is "relevant to virtually all archaeologists regardless of where they work."[11] The story fits within the myriad complex life patterns of Earth, as "[c]o-constitutive companion species and co-evolution are the rule, not the exception."[12] Although other animals also serve as companions, a debated designation, dogs are the ones labeled with the still-gender-exclusive title of "man's best friend."[13] Some dogs, along with just a few other species, eventually became "pets," a relatively new category for a companion species and one that is still problematic in its hierarchical, anthropocentric modality. The complexity of "pet" as a category is addressed in a later chapter.

What, then, does this shared human-canine story require of a new, ecofeminist history of the Christian tradition? In *The Companion Species Manifesto:*

Dogs, People, and Significant Otherness, Donna Haraway claims that studying dogs and culture is indeed a feminist enterprise as attested to by "those first mitochondrial canine bitches who got in the way of man making himself yet again in the Greatest Story Ever Told."[14] She continues, noting that "those bitches insisted on the history of companion species, a very mundane and ongoing sort of tale, one full of misunderstandings, achievements, crimes, and renewable hopes." In other words, when dogs are included in the human story, they might provide the ultimate example of the excluded other who is and always has been present. Recording official histories has been the privilege of the powerful. The stories of those without power often remain hidden. Certainly the histories of women and of the peasant classes rarely made it into official documents. Such is true for dogs as well, even though they have been a companion species to humans for thousands of years. Human history and canine history exist simultaneously and cannot be told without each other. Admitting canine history means admitting inclusive histories.

Dogs in the Pre-Christian Religious Mediterranean/ Mesopotamian Worlds

As an embedded aspect of human life for thousands of years, dogs obviously surface throughout human religious history as well. Often, however, finding this canine history requires looking beyond written texts and into visual depictions. It also requires a careful rereading of myths and stories. A few examples from the ancient Mediterranean religious world suffice as background to dogs as a "granted image" in Christian history.

Evidence from ancient Egypt suggests that, although not revered specifically as a deity, dogs did carry a certain amount of cultural clout and must have been valued companions. At least seventy-seven dogs from the Pharaonic period are known by name, and numerous dogs were mummified.[15] Herodotus, the Greek historian who visited Egypt in the fifth century BCE, noted that "if a dog dies they [the human family] shave the whole body and head. . . . All persons bury their dogs in sacred burial places in the towns where they belong."[16] At times the dog and the jackal are conflated in Egyptian language and imagery, but the jackal (not the dog) is associated with the lord of the dead, Anubis. Still, images of dogs on funerary structures abound throughout ancient Egypt and often seem to be pictures of the actual dog companion of the interred human. Another interesting link suggests that Anubis and Hermes (or Mercury), the Greek/Roman gods of transport, morphed into Hermanubis, "Mercury with a dog head."[17] Hermanubis might also have ties to the Christian saint, Christopher.

In Zoroastrianism, an ancient tradition that was also the state religion for several Persian empires, dogs figure centrally in death rites. Zoroastrianism understands the soul to "hover around the body for three days" after death, a common theme in the ancient Mediterranean world and one on which Christianity plays in certain ways later. Prayers accompany the soul, and a "dog is brought to 'gaze' upon the body" in a rite known as *sagdid*. This gazing confirms that the body is dead because dogs "have the power of discerning between life and death."[18] In addition, supernatural dogs guard the underground river and the "Chinvat Bridge," which spans the abyss of hell and leads to paradise.[19]

Another cultural site that moves research into the more immediate geographical area of the birth of Christianity is Ashkelon, the location of over twenty ancient cities covering a span of at least five thousand years (from 3,500 BCE to 1,500 CE), which sits on the Mediterranean Sea west of Jerusalem. Some amazing finds relate to dogs and their burial, as noted by archeologist Lawrence Stager: "Till now, we have found more than 700 partial or complete dog carcasses from the fifth century BC, most of them buried in the western half of Grid 50. Because only the eastern limits of the cemetery have been established, we can speculate that it was originally much larger, with dog burials probably numbering in the thousands. This is by far the largest animal cemetery of any kind known in the ancient world." (Stager later corrects this statement: "by far the largest dog cemetery known in the ancient world.")[20]

Other researchers indicate that "each dog burial seems to have been a discrete event."[21] At least 60 percent of the dogs were puppies, leading Stager to suggest "the concern for proper burial of what in some cases were probably dog fetuses reflects an intense relationship between dogs and humans."[22] From these findings, he concludes "the Ashkelon dogs were revered as sacred animals. As such, they were probably associated with a particular deity and with that god's sacred precinct, about which the dogs were free to roam."[23] Although this phenomenon seems to be short-lived, maybe only fifty years or so, it indicates that dogs occupied a central position in the religious life of this diverse ancient population during a time when Persians, Phoenicians, Greeks, Jews, and Egyptians traveled through or lived in the vicinity of Ashkelon.

In addition to the mummification of dogs in Egypt and the Ashkelon cemetery, dog burials exist throughout the rest of the ancient Mediterranean world:

> The ceremonial relationship between humans and canids in the eastern Mediterranean is found first in the Natufian deposits . . . where the burial of an old

woman was accompanied by a wolf or dog puppy. Closer in time to the Ashkelon
deposit, Levy reports two articulated dog burials with accompanying grave
good at the site of Gilat, a Chalcolithic cemetery. One of the authors examined
the burials "in situ," noting that both the burials and the animals were like the
Ashkelon inhumations. Levy suggests that the tradition of dog interment may
be more continuous than imagined. This is certainly the case in Egypt, where
a survey by Bonnet et al. (1989) reveals that complete dog skeletons were found
with human burials as early as the Neolithic and as far south as the Sudan.[24]

For example, one site includes thirty-three dog burials in a ramp leading
to the temple of the goddess of healing, Ninisina (Lady of Isin) or Gula, in
southern Mesopotamia. Dogs are linked to Gula from the second and first
millennia BCE; archeological evidence suggests that dog cults and healing
rites connect during that time frame. Isin, a city in the fertile crescent and the
capital of an ancient Semitic kingdom, contains some of the most convincing
of the Ninisina/Gula images of dogs and religion. Excavations of Isin and
the Gula temple complex reveal the obvious dog-goddess link. A portion of
her temple, built around 1050 BCE, includes the skeletons mentioned above,
along with "sheets of worked bronze with depictions of dogs; clay and bronze
figurines of dogs," and a "figure of a kneeling human embracing a dog."[25] In
texts from the period, the dog also functions as a messenger sent by Gula
and is "sworn by in oaths."[26] Interestingly, the same healing-dog connection
occurs later in Christian history, as shown below with such saints as Roch.

Arguably the best-known dog of the ancient world is Hades' guardian,
Cerberus. This creature stood at the entrance to underworld in Greek religious mythology, allowing people to enter but never allowing them to leave.
Cerberus is most often described as a three-headed dog, though he did have
parts from other creatures as well, such as a dragon's tail.[27] Orpheus and Heracles (Latin, Hercules) both encountered Cerberus. While Heracles fought
him and dragged him to the surface of the earth, ending up with wounds
from Cerberus, Orpheus simply lulled the dog to sleep with his music. These
mythological encounters might suggest something about ways for humans (or
human-gods) to relate to dogs effectively without getting bitten by them.

So dogs loom large in various ancient Mediterranean and Mesopotamian
religious cultures as servants in temples, companions in death, messengers
of the goddess, and healers. But human-dog relationships in these ancient
cultures are ambivalent at best. In addition to the above-mentioned sacred
roles they filled, dogs appear as nuisances, as unclean animals (along with
swine), and are sometimes used as sacrifices, unless considered too impure
for this function. For example, evidence indicates that Robigalia, a spring
festival in central Italy, included the sacrifice of dogs, usually "red dogs . . .

to placate the Dog Star which is inimical to crops."[28] In Etruscan cultures of the same period, the fertility goddess is "placated with the blood and entrails of a suckling puppy" in order to avoid ruination of the crops.[29]

Various attitudes come through in ancient Hebrew and early Christian texts as well. Often the positions revealed by the texts of these two traditions mirror basic attitudes of the cultures during the historical periods when they were written. Thus, as Walter Houston points out, the "dog was a universal scavenger, a consumer of blood, dead flesh, and dubious things, and references to it in the Hebrew Bible are consistently unfavourable; its name is an all-purpose insult."[30] For example, in Psalm 22:20 the psalmist pleas, "Deliver my soul from the sword, my life from the power of the dog!" And according to Isaiah 56, dogs are condemned for their "mighty appetite; they never have enough."[31] This position is verified by stories such as that of Jezebel, who, after she was killed by being hoisted out the window, was eaten by dogs, leaving nothing to bury except her skull, feet, and the palms of her hands (2 Kings 33–37). But Elaine Goodfriend's research into the Hebrew word *keleb* in Deuteronomy 23:19 suggests that dogs in the ancient Near East seem "to have been viewed as a service animal (for guarding and hunting), to the extent that 'canine' became synonymous with faithful service."[32] She continues by stressing that the canine, while occupying a role in Israel's pastoral economy and being one of the only animals encountered on a daily basis by humans at the time, was still "distinguished . . . by its status as a carnivorous scavenger and predator."[33]

Early Christianity maintains this association between dogs and impurity. According to the Gospel of Matthew, Jesus says, "Do not give dogs what is holy" (Matt. 7:6). The early Christian pedagogical text, *The Didache,* echoes this theme in reference to the eucharist and baptism: "Let no one eat or drink of your eucharist save those who have been baptized in the name of the Lord, since the Lord has said, "Do not give what is holy to the dogs" (9:5).[34] This text most likely uses dogs as a metaphor for those humans who are not baptized or are, in some other way, deemed unworthy to receive the Eucharist. As a matter of fact, this connection between dogs and the Eucharist surfaces again in Last Supper visual imagery addressed below. But metaphors carry weight in their very image and interpretation; therefore, in representing dogs as those who are unworthy, the connection sticks.

The other story in the canonical gospels that references dogs lends itself to various interpretations:

> From there he [Jesus] set out and went away to the region of Tyre. He entered a house and did not want anyone to know he was there. Yet he could not escape

notice, but a woman whose little daughter had an unclean spirit immediately heard about him, and she came and bowed down at his feet. Now the woman was a Gentile, of Syrophoenician origin. She begged him to cast the demon out of her daughter. He said to her, "Let the children be fed first, for it is not fair to take the children's food and throw it to the dogs." But she answered him, "Sir, even the dogs under the table eat the children's crumbs." Then he said to her, "For saying that, you may go—the demon has left your daughter." (Mark 7:24–29)

Undoubtedly this incident refers to the distinction between Gentiles (the Syrophoenician woman) and Jews, with dogs representing the Gentiles. Here the "other" (the woman) challenges Jesus when he calls Gentiles "dogs." But she sees through his rhetoric to the deeper truth Jesus conceals. This pattern repeats itself through the Gospel of Mark as Jesus' disciples and family members fail to understand his teachings but "others" often do understand. Jesus meets the woman's challenge and rewards her for it; she understands that even dogs (and in this case the Greek word used for "dog" refers to a "pet" or "small dog") do get to eat the crumbs. So the total other, be they canine or human, comes under the umbrella of compassion in Jesus' teachings.

Another rather ambiguous parable in the canonical gospel of Luke describes "a poor man named Lazarus, full of sores." While he begged for scraps from the rich man's table, "dogs came and licked his sores" (Luke 16:20–21). On the one hand, the description of dogs licking his sores connects Lazarus to even more misery and to the lowest possible state of existence. On the other hand, connections to the healing capacities of dogs recognized in ancient Near Eastern cultures also might be involved in this parable. Later Christian visual art tells this story frequently, and dogs figure prominently in the depictions.

Finally, the Arabic Infancy Gospel, a later text not included in the canon, reports another encounter between Jesus and a dog. A boy who was "tormented by Satan . . . used to bite all who came near him." When the boy's mother brings him to Mary and the young Jesus, he "wished to bite the Lord Jesus, but was not able." Though the reasons are unclear, after the boy tried to bite and then hit Jesus, "Satan went forth out of that boy . . . in the shape of a dog."[35] Interestingly, the boy, named Judas, grows up to be one of Jesus' disciples, the one who eventually betrays him. Dogs may not fare well in the presence of Jesus, though this is still debatable and the evidence is scarce.

The presence of dogs with humans over countless generations and thousands or tens of thousands of years points to their diverse reflection in human religious traditions as well. Dogs are variously faithful, powerful, and positive; they are also unclean, symbols of the other that must be banished, or simply a nuisance. But the presence of dogs as an aspect of the religious world is incontrovertible. Now we turn to their particular presence in the history of the Christian tradition. Again, it will prove to be a mixed picture, but their very "grantedness" speaks volumes to the role of the human-dog relationship.

Peter and the Preaching Dog

As mentioned in an earlier chapter, early Christian apocryphal works contain a wealth of information about animals, real and symbolic, in Christian history. One dog story from the Acts of Peter stands out. Peter traveled to Rome and proceeded to contest Simon Magus, the infamous early Christian heretic. When he, and the large crowd that followed, approached the house of Marcellus, where Simon was staying, the doorkeeper turned Peter away. But Peter addressed the crowd and told them they would "see a great and marvelous wonder." Here, the dog enters the story:

> And Peter, seeing a great dog tied fast with a massive chain, went up to him and let him loose. And when the dog was let loose he acquired a human voice and said to Peter, "What do you bid me do, you servant of the ineffable living God?" And Peter said to him, "Go in and tell Simon in the presence of his company, 'Peter says to you, Come out in public; for on your account I have come to Rome, you wicked man and troubler of simple souls.'" And immediately the dog ran and went in and rushed into the middle of Simon's companions and lifting his fore-feet called out with a loud voice, "(I tell) you Simon, Peter the servant of Christ is standing at the door, and says to you, 'Come out in public; for on your account I have come to Rome, you most wicked deceiver of simple souls.'"[36]

Of course, the speaking dog renders Simon and Marcellus momentarily speechless, reversing the normal order of articulation between the species. Marcellus throws himself at Peter's feet, but Simon continues to counter the apostle and, for good measure, argues with the dog as well: "Peter, there is a huge contest between Simon and the dog which you sent; for Simon says to the dog, 'Say that I am not here'—but the dog says more to him than the message you gave; and when he finished the mysterious work which you gave him, he shall die at your feet." In this interesting, brief account, the hearer or reader learns that the dog "says more" than instructed by Peter, preaching the gospel against a heretic on his own. This canine embellishment argues for some comprehension of the religious message on the part of the dog. When challenged by Simon to deny his presence in the house, the dog responds:

> You most wicked and shameless (man), you enemy of all that live and believe in Christ Jesus, (here is) a dumb animal sent to you and taking a human voice to convict you and prove you a cheat and a deceiver. Have you thought for all these

hours, (only) to say, "Say that I am not here"? Were you not ashamed to raise your feeble and useless voice against Peter, the servant and apostle of Christ, as if you could hide from him who commanded me to speak against (you to) your face? And this is not for your sake, but for those whom you were perverting and sending to destruction. Cursed therefore you shall be, you enemy and corruptor of the way to the truth of Christ, who shall prove your iniquities which you have done with undying fire, and you shall be in outer darkness.[37]

The dog then returned to Peter, reported on his words, and told Peter that he would have a great contest with "Simon, the enemy of Christ." He also predicts that the confrontation between the apostle and the heretic will "convert many to the faith that were deceived by him." Thus the dog is transformed from a beast on a leash, to a servant of Peter, to a preacher-prophet. Of course, he must then lie down at the feet of Peter and die.

It seems that a dog with a voice cannot live for too long in Christian history but enters the story at a central point and serves God faithfully. While keeping in mind the tension between symbolism and reality, the story provides a clear entry into the human-dog relational world. Though not categorized as a martyr in this account, the story suggests that the dog's acts of proclamation require his death. Dogs, a constant presence, can be servants of the divine and do become such, even servants to the point of sacrificial death.

Dogs: Here, There and Everywhere in Christian Imagery

In his book *The Pawprints of History,* Stanley Coren states, "Perhaps the contributions of dogs to history go unnoticed simply because they are too commonplace."[38] The same could be said for Christian visual presentations. If one begins paying close attention to the art adorning Christian churches, particularly those built during the Middle Ages and the Renaissance, dogs are everywhere. Sometimes they are heavily laden with symbol, but other times they are simply granted, they are naturally, unassumingly there, and in terms of historical research, they have often been taken for granted. In other words, dogs are present in myriad Christian texts—visual, written, oral—because they cannot not be present. Because of their omnipresence in human culture, they cannot be absent from Christianity's visual representations. Below I focus on dogs in a specific setting—around the table with Jesus—but first a glance at dogs in various other Christian images.

The Basilica Dei Santi Giovanni e Paolo might not be the first church one visits in Venice—the Basilica of San Marco captures that honor—but the artwork of this Dominican church, the burial place of many doges, is replete with dogs. A small brown dog witnesses the baptism of Jesus and a brown-

and-white dog curls in the corner as St. Giacinto walks on water to bring the holy sacrament safely across a river.[39] By far the most striking collection of subtle dog images is in the Cappella di San Domenico, a chapel adorned by five low-relief bronze pieces of Guiseppe Mazza. In these Episodes from the Life of St. Dominic, a dog rides in the boat with the saint and, later, peeks out from under the saintly robes as a witness to St. Dominic's death. It should be noted here that dogs are closely connected with the Dominican order as a whole and often accompany Dominicans in visual imagery as "Domini canes"; thus the linguistic link to the order and possibly the reason that dogs are present in the episodes from the saint's life.

Another striking example of dogs and Dominicans is Andrea di Bonaiuto's *Via Veritatis,* a thirty-foot-high fresco adorning the Spanish Chapel of Santa Maria Novella in Florence.[40] The black-and-white dogs guard the sheep, who sit in front of the pope, and they attack wolves that might endanger the faith-

Death of St. Dominic by Mazza, Venice, Italy. Photo taken by author; courtesy of the Cultural Ministry of Venice.

ful, symbolized by the sheep. At least ten *Domini canes* line the base of the fresco, following orders from Saint Dominic himself to serve as guards.

Another interesting image of a dog with the saint is in the Church of San Nicolai in Treviso. In the front of the sanctuary, on the altar, is a statue of St. Dominic. Next to him is a small dog standing against his left leg. As I researched this particular statue, asking the caretaker of the church about the artist and the subject, the caretaker responded that he had never really taken much notice of the dog but commented that the canine's presence was simply part of St. Dominic's iconography so taken for granted at the statue's feet.

Dogs at the Table with Jesus?

A cat curls up to warm herself by the roaring kitchen fire as a small dog licks food remnants off of the plates, a servant kneels down by the fire listening to instructions. Something important takes place and someone of great significance eats in their midst. Pietro Lorenzetti pays unprecedented attention to the happenings in this small room to the side of the main event, the Last Supper, in his fresco of the same name adorning the Basilica of San Francesco's Lower Church in Assisi, Italy. Art historian Millard Meiss describes this groundbreaking work:

> For the first time a painter envisaged with considerable consistency a space illuminated by a light within it. The wood fire in the chimney brightens almost everything in the kitchen. . . . Most extraordinary of all, the cat and the dog, very close to the source of this light, throw shadows on the floor. The shadows were not painted onto the fresco surface but are contained within it, so they are beyond doubt original. . . . It is interesting that these shadows appear close to a brilliant light and are associated with animals. No sacred figure in any of the scenes cast shadows. At this time such shadows belong, as the reproduction shows, to a "slice of life" that is governed by a different mode of seeing.[41]

As they congregate to beg for scraps from every table, dogs begin to gather with Jesus and the disciples in images of *The Last Supper*. Some hide, some draw the eye immediately at center stage, some curl in sleep, and others eat or drink; cats sometimes accompany dogs in these images.

The earliest relationships between humans and dogs, as mentioned previously, were probably created and cemented around food. These two species continue to connect with food serving as a powerful intermediary. In order to simply survive, dogs perfected the art of gathering scraps from the eating spaces of humans or convinced humans to share their meals; likewise humans convinced dogs to guard livestock, which became food, or hunt wild animals

The Last Supper. by Lorenzetti, Assisi, Italy. Photo taken by author; courtesy of the Basilica of St. Francis, Assisi.

for human consumption. Martin Luther even writes about dogs and food in *Table Talk.* Tolpel, Luther's dog, is mentioned frequently, and the reformer admired the ability of his canine companion to focus: "Oh, if I could only pray the way this dog watches the meat! All his thoughts are concentrated on the piece of meat. Otherwise he has no thought, wish, or hope."[42] So dogs at the Last Supper just make common sense as they would have been present wherever food was being trapped, raised, fed, killed, and served. A watchdog, most likely, worked with the shepherd guarding the lamb that provided part of the Passover meal that became the Last Supper in the Christian story. They were connected to the process of preparing the Last Supper from the beginning. But I suggest that a deeper sense of requisite other-species companionship is at play as evidenced in the images described here.

Some art historians, and perhaps the artists themselves, interpret the inclusion of dogs in images of the Last Supper for the reason stated earlier: Dogs represent those who are not worthy to receive the Eucharist. As the Last

Supper evolves into the first Eucharist in Christian liturgical symbolism, only those deemed worthy to receive are welcome, a major point of theological debate throughout Christian history. If the eucharistic table is not open to all participants, then worshipers, those viewing these liturgical images thus those for whom the symbols were included, must be reminded that some are barred from the table; thus the dogs are the banished ones. Indeed, this might be part of the reason for the presence of dogs, but I suggest that it is neither the only nor the most significant reason.

Upon entering the Sistine Chapel, one's eyes are trained to find Michelangelo's overwhelming *Last Judgment*, but the chapel's interior contains other images as well, including Cosimo Rosselli's *Last Supper*, painted between 1482 and 1483. It bears several traditional iconographic details, including a young John seated next to Jesus and a confrontational Judas, with a small impish devil on his shoulder, across the table from Jesus. Interestingly, though Jesus breaks the bread and has a chalice in front of him, no other food or beverage images sit on the table. This imagery differs dramatically from Lorenzetti's depiction, with its earthy portrayal that includes the kitchen, servants, and animals of the household. Interpretations of the role played by the dog and cat vary. Mancinelli states that although the symbolism in the image as a whole is called "quite traditional," the "two animals in the foreground" are an "exception" to that imagery.[43] However, the presence of animals, particularly dogs in Last Supper imagery, is anything but exceptional, just rarely noticed. Carol Lewine suggests that the "snarling cat and dog" who "square off at one another near the foreground of Rosselli's *Last Supper*" may have Eucharistic meaning and are placed to "attract the viewer's attention." She also points out that the presence of dogs in Last Supper scenes purposefully directs the viewer to Jesus' words in Matthew, "Do not give that which is holy to dogs," thus providing a warning to those who might be unworthy to receive the Eucharist.[44]

A third fascinating image from the early sixteenth century indicates a different role for dogs.[45] In this, one of Jacopo Bassano's early works (1537), the artist follows some standard iconographical patterns in his portrayal of the Last Supper, patterns paralleled in other works from the same period such as those of Bonifazio.[46] But there is one particularly striking difference when compared with other portrayals that include dogs. In this image, rather than assume a position of begging or of curling up under the table or confronting a cat, the dog is partaking of a meal. Someone has put a bowl of food or water on the floor for the dog. This is a rarely seen twist on the dog at the table as the canine really joins the fellowship of eating at the Last Supper. Bassano's other, and probably better known, *Last Supper* (1542) also includes a dog, though in this case the dog curls up by the washbasin in front of the table rather than sharing in the feast. A cat peers into the scene as well from the edge, possibly focusing on the resting dog. Though much action occurs around the table itself and it is suggested that the image portrays the moment when Jesus asks who will betray him, the dog is at peace, sleeping curled up under the bare feet of the disciples gathered at the table. He might even reflect the one reclining disciple directly above him.

Sometimes having dogs front and center might have led to shifting the designation of Last Supper images. Such may have been the case with Paolo Veronese's painting, currently titled *Feast in the House of Levi*. This painting was originally planned for the refectory of the church of Santi Giovanni e Paolo in Venice.[47] Veronese completed the painting in April 1573 and by July was "summoned before the Holy Tribunal to answer charges of indecorum in his large painting."[48] When asked by this inquisition to repair the painting, Veronese chose, rather, to rename it, thus removing the controversy over the presence of "buffoons, drunkards, Germans, and dwarfs" at the Last Supper.[49] Although dogs are not mentioned directly in this sixteenth century controversy, their presence cannot be denied because they are, again, placed with Jesus, St. Peter, and St. Paul under the central arch. One dog sits in front of the table looking back, possibly at the cat sliding out from underneath the tablecloth, or possibly at Jesus who looks down in his general direction.

The Last Supper by Bassano, Rome, Italy. Photo courtesy of Scala.

Feast in the House of Levi/Last Supper by Veronese, Venice, Italy. Photo by author; courtesy of L'Accademia, Venice.

Another dog can be seen walking behind the column, with his back to the viewer. But both are placed in close proximity to Jesus and to the table.

Another sixteenth-century Venetian artist, Jacopo Tintoretto, painted some ten versions of *The Last Supper*.[50] He incorporated dogs into at least four of these images.[51] About 1580, Tintoretto painted a large *Last Supper* for the Banco Del Sacramento of Santa Margherita in Venice. Since that time the painting has been relocated and it now hangs in San Stefano, another church in Venice. In this fabulous image a dog is front and center, positioned directly beneath the sacrificial lamb on the table and pointing the viewer to Jesus. Standing on the steps that lead to the table, the dog focuses on Jesus, who is serving bread to the disciples. A female figure, a child, and a male figure (possibly a beggar) are also positioned on or at the base of the stairs, and their bodies flow in the same direction as that of the dog. Thomas Worthen connects the woman and the dog: "The dog before her, presented with such emblematic clarity, alludes to the story of Christ and the Canaanite woman (Matt. 15:22–28): When she importuned him, he answered and said, It is not meet to take the children's bread, and to cast it to dogs. And she said, Truth, Lord: yet the dogs eat of the crumbs which fall from their masters' table."

The significance of the woman is less certain than that of the dog. . . . In any event she and the dog together seem to represent faith and the love of God."[52] So rather than symbolizing those excluded from the table, this dog might represent faith and the love of God, a significant shift indeed.

Tintoretto's *Last Supper,* painted for for the Scuola Grande di San Rocco, includes a much more "agitated" dog, but one that is also approaching the table and positioned on the stairs in the center of the painting.[53] David Rosand, in his study of Tintoretto, describes the scene: "Seated below the steps that elevate the setting of the mensa, and clearly belonging to a world beyond the historical moment of Christ's supper, two beggars patiently await that charity. Between them and the prominently displayed bread and bowl and pitcher, a dog noses his way back into the sacred space, a canine foil to the Eucharistic fare: 'Ecce, panis angelorum . . . non mittendus canibus.'"[54] Rosand's reference here is significant to the study of dogs at the Last Supper. Thomas Aquinas, in his liturgy for the Feast of Corpus Christi, includes those same Latin lines: "Behold the bread of Angels, denied to dogs."[55] Although this could be part of the reason dogs are present at the table, examining more images and the position of dogs in these images suggests otherwise.

An earlier version of *The Last Supper* painted by Tintoretto for San Simeon Grande in the 1560s shares the depiction of the woman and dog together, though this time the dog is positioned at the side instead of the center. But

The Last Supper by Tintoretto, Scuolo Grande di San Rocco, Venice. Photo by author; courtesy of Scuolo Grande di San Rocco.

the portrayal is prominent, a large figure, and the dog focuses directly on the table again, as in the Santa Margherita piece. This dog appears comfortable in the setting and, while watching everything that goes on around the room, is still at peace positioned on the floor as part of the congregation gathered around the table. Tintoretto includes a similar dog in *The Washing of the Feet* (1547).[56] Here the dog lies in the center of the painting, immediately behind Jesus, regarding him as he washes the feet of the disciples. In this portrayal the dog could almost be interpreted as either the companion of Jesus or at least a mirror image of service to others that Jesus enacts. In other words, the dog appears to be both symbol (faithful service) and real, the dog that follows the Christ.

And, perchance, other dogs follow the Christ to find their feast. Although not as common as images of dogs present at the Last Supper, they do show up in other scenes involving sacred meals. For example, the story of Christ feeding the masses, the miracle of the loaves and fishes, is one of the most widely told. This account is included, with variations of course, in all four canonical gospels (Mark 6:30–44, Matthew 14:13–21, Luke 9:10–17, John 6:1–13). It is also widely represented in art, though not as frequently as the Last Supper. Occasionally dogs join the throngs to share in the miracle feast, as portrayed by Santi di Tito at the Church of Santo Spirito in Florence. On one side of the image a young man points to Jesus, directing the eyes of the people gathered at the miracle occurring. Mirroring him is a child who looks at a small brown-and-white dog; the dog looks up at the child. Just as the young man tells the humans to witness the miracle, so the boy directs the gaze of the dog to the miracle. The dog is invited to run and join the feast.

Dogs and Saints

> One day a guest came to Dubthach's house. Her [Brigit's] father entrusted her with a good piece of bacon to be boiled for the guest. She gave one-fifth of the bacon to a hungry dog which approached her. When the dog had eaten this, she gave it another fifth. The guest, who was watching, remained silent as though overcome with sleep. On returning home again the father found his daughter. "Have you boiled the food well?" he asked. "Yes," she said. And he himself counted the pieces of bacon and found them all there. Then the guest told Dubthach what the girl had done. "After this," said Dubthach "she performed more miracles than can be told." Then that portion of food was distributed among the poor.[57]

The Irish Life of Brigit includes numerous animal stories, but few as touching as the stories of her compassion for and hospitality to the village dogs of

The Washing of the Feet by Tintoretto, Museo del Prado, Madrid, Spain. Photo courtesy of Scala.

Christ Feeding the Masses with St. Gervase and St. Protase by Santi di Tito. Photo courtesy of Alinari Archives.

Ireland. And, it seems, God protects the dogs and Brigit from repercussions by miraculously restoring the food she has shared. Lisa Bitel suggests that the miracle story of the hungry dog was likely reenacted on Brigit's feast day because hagiographies serve as liturgical drama, not simply or only as prose. "So when Brigit was cooking bacon in a big cauldron and looked a dolefully hungry dog in the eye," she notes, "it was meant to be a crowd-pleasing scene shared by her loving devotees." The dog, symbol of the most downtrodden but also a real dog, served to remind the pilgrims of "Jesus' own miracles."[58] I suggest that the dog might even be representative of Jesus in disguise, referencing Matthew 25: "Lord when was it that we saw you hungry and gave you food. . . . Truly I tell you, just as you did it to one of the least of these who are members of my family, you did it to me."

According to *The Golden Legend,* St. Christopher was "a Canaanite by birth, a man of prodigious size—he was twelve feet tall—and fearsome of visage."[59] His story combines travel, martyrdom, encounters with the devil, and the act of bearing the Christ-child across a swollen river, thus the designation "Christophoros, the Christ-bearer." During the Middle Ages gazing upon the saint kept one safe from death for that day, and thus his iconography was popular. But his iconography tells even more about this saint, whose name before baptism was Reprobus or "outcast." Whereas most Western imagery of Christopher highlights his action as Christ-bearer, and thus one finds portrayals of him as a giant carrying a child on his shoulders, Eastern imagery focuses on Christopher as cynocephalic, having a dog's head. Because of his designation as a "Canaanite," thus an outsider, and as "fearsome of visage," his dog's head could have easily been connected to these attributes. Also, there are probable links between the dog-headed Christopher and Hermanubis, a god of healing whose tradition comes from both Egyptian and Hellenistic sources. Icons of St. Christopher with a dog's head date to the reign of Justinian, found in a monastery of Mount Sinai, and continue throughout Eastern Orthodox history. He's also mentioned as dog-headed in the apocryphal Gnostic text, the Acts of Bartholomew.[60] An eighteenth-century Greek Orthodox hymn recognizes him as "St. Christopher, dog-headed, valiant in faith, fervent in prayer."[61] So although the iconography of Christopher as dog-headed is rare in Catholic Christianity and the saint has even been removed from the church's universal calendar (as of 1969), the very fact of his portrayal remains intriguing.

Saint Roch and his dog are another story altogether, one portrayed in artwork throughout European churches. Roch is easily identified because he is usually carrying a pilgrim's staff or walking stick, his leg is oftentimes wounded, and he is almost always accompanied by a dog who carries a loaf of bread in his mouth. The hagiographical accounts of Roch tell of a person who fearlessly aids people dying from the plague. His tale follows a relatively standard template: he is born into wealth, consecrated from birth; he leaves riches to seek a holy life; and he ministers to the sick and dying in various hospitals during the awful onsets of the plague. But another character enters the story, a dog "which in all his pilgrimage had faithfully attended him."[62] When Roch himself is stricken by the plague, he chooses to leave and die alone in the woods rather than infect other people. At this point the dog begins feeding him, leaving for the city each day and returning with a loaf of bread. Roch's relics eventually find a home in Venice; his iconography fills a number of Venetian churches.

Saint Guinefort

One of the most fascinating martyr-saints is Saint Guinefort. The stories of his heroic martyrdom and of the healings that took place at his shrine influenced generations of believers in southern France. Guinefort, a trusted dog, was left alone with an infant. When the father returned, he saw blood covering the room and surrounding the infant's crib. Guinefort sat next to the crib, blood around his mouth. Immediately the man took an arrow and shot Guinefort in the heart. Approaching the crib, he saw that his child was unharmed. Below the crib was the body of a dead snake who had been trying to get to the infant. Guinefort had saved the child's life.

The template for the legend of Guinefort is relatively common and includes these characteristics: a faithful dog is left to watch over an infant, usually a male child who is heir to the elite parent's wealth and power; while the mother, father, and (sometimes) nurse are gone, another animals (usually, though not always, a snake) enters the room; the dog fights off the intruder, suffering injuries; when other guardians return, the blood-covered dog stands by the infant and it is assumed that the dog has attacked the child; the "lord" kills the dog; then all discover that the dog actually saved the life of the child. In many European versions of the story a prominent burial site for the dog concludes the story. This tale appears in the traditions of India from as early as the sixth century BCE in the Sanskrit *Panchatantra;* it also moves through Greek legend in a slightly different form and is found in a medieval Hebrew text (translated into Latin by John of Capua during the thirteenth century).[63] Interestingly, an almost identical legend emerges in Welsh folklore and might lead to the Welsh proverb "To repent as deeply as the man who killed his dog."[64] This legend, also from the thirteenth century, tells of Prince Llywelyn the Great, his son Dafydd, and Cylart, the greyhound (or wolfhound) left to guard the child. Eventually the dog's name shifted to "Gelert" and a rather famous poem was penned about Gelert's grave.[65]

The primary textual traditions about Saint Guinefort come from *De Adoratione guinefortis Canis* recorded by Étienne de Bourbon (c. 1180–1262), a Dominican inquisitor. These anecdotes were used by preachers in sermons, but Étienne claims their authenticity. First he sets the story of Guinefort in the context of "supersticionibus contumeliosis," offensive or insulting superstitions, some of which are insulting to God, others to humans. The ones associated with Guinefort are offensive to the divine. He also connected these to the "wretched women sorcerers" who take their children to elder trees for healing and, he suggests, worship these trees and "ant-hills." With this introduction, loaded with its many intertwining characters, he proceeds to tell the specific story of Saint Guinefort. The entire exempla is included here because of the prevalence of this particular tale in Western history and its appearance within a central Christianized saint and heretic setting:

> This recently happened in the diocese of Lyons where, when I preached against the reading of oracles, and was hearing confession, numerous women confessed that they had taken their children to Saint Guinefort. As I thought that this was some holy person, I continued with my enquiry and finally learned that this was actually a greyhound, which had been killed in the following manner. . . . One day, when the lord and lady had gone out of the house and the nurse had done likewise, leaving the baby alone in the cradle, a huge serpent entered the house and approached the baby's cradle. Seeing this, the greyhound, which had remained behind, chased the serpent and, attacking it beneath the cradle, upset the cradle and bit the serpent all over, which defended itself, biting the dog equally severely. Finally, the dog killed it and threw it away from the cradle. The cradle, the floor, the dog's mouth and head were all drenched in the serpent's blood. Although badly hurt by the serpent, the dog remained on guard beside the cradle. When the nurse came back and saw all this she thought that the dog had devoured the child, and let out a scream of misery. Hearing it the child's mother also ran up, looked, thought the same thing and screamed too. Likewise the knight, when he arrived, thought the same thing and drew his sword and killed the dog. Then, when they went closer to the baby they found it safe and sound, sleeping peacefully. Casting around for some explanation, they discovered the serpent, torn to pieces by the dog's bites, and now dead. Realising then the true facts of the matter, and deeply regretting having unjustly killed so useful a dog they threw it into a well in front of the manor door, threw a great pile of stones on top of it, and planted trees beside it, in memory of the event. Now, by divine will, the manor was destroyed and the estate, reduced to a desert, was abandoned by its inhabitants. But the peasants, hearing of the dog's conduct and of how it had been killed, although innocent, and for a deed

for which it might have expected praise, visited the place, honoured the dog as
a martyr, prayed to it when they were sick or in need of something.[66]

Étienne determines that the dog must be labeled a heretic, so he has Guinefort "disinterred, and the sacred wood cut down and burnt, along with the
remains of the dog." Records vary, but some indicate that sick children were
brought to the dog's shrine until the nineteenth century. Saint Guinefort, a
martyr, received the popular designation of "saint," a title usually reserved
for human animals. Apparently a dog cannot be an official saint, though he
can be an official heretic. Indeed, as Schmitt maintains, Étienne de Bourbon
never doubts the "diabolic nature" of the dog.[67]

Those venerating Guinefort are Christian, or at least it appears that the
common practitioners are Christian, though certainly pre-Christian elements
remain within the population. Also important to recall is the process through
which a person (or a dog) becomes a saint. Through the first thousand years
of Christianity designations of "sainthood" took place on a relatively local
level with bishops in control of the process. This allowed for morphing of
pagan figures, arguably many including such figures as Brigit in Ireland, into
saints. But in the year 1234, during the same period when Étienne de Bourbon
inquires about St. Guinefort, the Decretals of Pope Gregory IX incorporate
designations of sainthood into the general law of the church. In other words,
from that point forward only the pope could canonize a saint.[68] But the local people, in the form of their own popular religion, continue to venerate
Guinefort for generations after the incident with the Dominican inquisitor.
The greyhound remains a saint and a healer regardless of the position of the
hierarchical powers.

Dogs as Demons and Heretics

Because they are so often our companions, projecting images of evil on
dogs, thus displacing evil from ourselves, is a common practice. As the most
prominent "other" species in some form of relationship with humans over
thousands of years, dogs become easy scapegoats. So they, along with cats, are
demonized in some cases. Recall the devil being sent from Judas into the dog
in one of the apocryphal gospels mentioned above; recall that dogs in scenes
of the Last Supper often symbolize those who are not worthy. So dog, the
other, bears the weight of projected evil through the history of Christianity.
Not only was the saint, Guinefort, transformed by the official church into a
heretic, but other dogs become symbols of the evil inherent in the world.

In Martin Luther's *Table Talk* the following account indicates that dogs
remained symbolic (and real) heretics into the period of the Reformation:

The doctor [Martin Luther] said, "I just received a letter from Jonas. He wrote that a dog had shit into the grave of the bishop of Halle. I believe it's fatal, for it has also happened to others before. Once when there was a procession with banners around a church, the verger put the holy water pot on the ground. A dog came along and pissed into the holy water pot. A priest noticed this because he was sprinkling the water, and he said, 'You impious dog! Have you become a Lutheran too?'"[69]

For different Christians, the very same dog can be a heretic or a hero.

Some graphic images of dogs as symbolic of the devil emerge during the long periods of witchcraft scares and instances of mass possession throughout Europe (and later the North American colonies) from the late fifteenth century until the late nineteenth century. This example from the Netherlands is typical:

> During a mass possession in a convent in Hessenberg (near Nijmegen, Spanish Netherlands), the demons "played so sweetly upon the lyre and the cithara that the maidens might easily have been induced to dance in chorus. Then, in the form of a dog, he would leap into the bed of one of the nuns and the suspicion would fall upon her of having committed the 'silent sin'" (masturbation). In another convent, near Cologne, another demon in the shape of a dog penetrated inside the nuns' inner garments, and the movements of their habits "gave indications of a sordid sexual skirmish," while demons in the shape of cats did the same in yet another convent, this one at Hensberg in the duchy of Cleves.[70]

This complex sociological event involves issues of bestiality, gender, authority, and mendicancy versus cloistered orders, to name just a few of the issues. Regardless, dogs figure prominently as the physical embodiment of evil.

The late Middle Ages and early Renaissance period also signal a shift in the visual imagery of Jesus' crucifixion. Psalm 22 becomes a major source for this change in the Passion narrative because the opening words of the Psalm, "My God, my God, why have you forsaken me?" provide the intertextual connection between the Hebrew Scriptures and the crucifixion accounts in both Matthew and Mark. Later in Psalm 22, bulls, lions, and dogs enter the lament and torture the psalmist and are thus interpreted as torturers of Jesus as well. With a refocus on the Passion narrative in both the art and literature of the later Middle Ages, dogs enter the scene as tormenters of Jesus.[71] It should be noted that dogs probably played a part in the awful history of crucifixion. John Dominic Crossan points out that "what we often forget about crucifixion is the carrion crow and scavenger dog who respectively croak above and growl below the dead or dying body."[72] Still, this portrayal is significantly different compared to dogs curled up at the feet of the disciples during the Last Supper.

In his study of animal categories and taboo, Edmund Leach makes another interesting connection between dogs and heresy. He points out that in English, "dog" and "God" must be understood as linguistic inversions; thus they are employed as actual inversions as well. So in the seventeenth century witchcraft trials in England, "it was very commonly asserted that the Devil appeared in the form of a Dog—that is, God backwards."[73]

Conclusion

"Taking a dog to church" happens each day at St. Anne's Episcopal Church in Morrison, Illinois. Norman Kolenbrander, one of the "faithful" members of the community, attends morning prayer there each day, along with Father Gary and his two dogs, Brigid and Bega (named after two fifth-century Irish nuns). According to Kolenbrander, these two dogs participate fully in the service. "As I enter the sanctuary," he states, "they offer greeting, happily placing their paws on my shoulders. . . . As I kneel in a prayer of preparation, they often bestow the blessing of a holy kiss. . . . Father Gary reads the scripture lessons, Brigid often sits in a dignified posture beside him; with her black coat and white throat patch, she looks as clerical as her master." He even recalls one morning when the two dogs performed a type of impromptu liturgical drama. Father Gary read a passage from the book of Romans describing the chaos of a society that turns its back on God. In the midst of this "Brigid and Began began biting and snarling and whirling in a circle around the lectern. . . . I could not choke back an awareness of that reality that two members of our congregation had so generously helped illustrate—a world in disarray."[74] These two canine worship companions participate and perform; in this setting human-dog connections continue as they have for countless generations. Dogs are simply and fully present as humans go about their lives.

Donna Haraway's ideas illuminate here again. Dogs, she notes, "in their historical complexity, matter here. Dogs are not an alibi for other themes; dogs are fleshly material-semiotic presences in the body of technoscience."[75] Dogs also matter in Christian hagiography, iconography, and ritual. They are always, everywhere portrayed, accompanying saints, acting as saints, eating meals, "being" evil, hovering at the foot of the cross, and signifying healing. A complete history of the Christian tradition must include the place of canines, one of the ignored others whose impact cannot be denied.

6. Animals Return to the Sanctuary

Blessings of Animals in Contemporary American Culture

> In the name of St. Francis and the many other holy people all over
> the world throughout time who love and cherish animals, I bless
> you and this shelter. May the people who meet you here know that
> you matter to the One who created you and may they greet you
> and care for you in that Spirit.[1]

Blessings of the animals/pets entered the mainstream U.S. cultural scene in the latter part of the twentieth century. Although blessings of various animals took place in different times and places, and for varying reasons, throughout Christian history, the growth of these rituals beginning in the late twentieth century is dramatic. Most likely inspired by the service at the Cathedral of St. John the Divine in New York City, addressed specifically below, they spread to numerous Christian congregations of different denominations, to interfaith settings, and even into the secular world. By the early twenty-first century, hundreds, if not thousands, of these blessings take place annually. Because of this rapid growth and the significance of public ritual, I suggest that a cultural shift regarding animals, inaugurated by myriad factors, marks this time period. What that shift entails is complex and contested, but blessings point to it.

In his seminal work *The Interpretation of Cultures,* Clifford Geertz defines the central role of ritual in society:

> For it is in ritual—that is, consecrated behavior—that this conviction that religious conceptions are veridical and that religious directives are sound is somehow generated. It is in some sort of ceremonial form—even if that form be hardly more than the recitation of a myth, the consultation of an oracle, or the decoration of a grave—that the moods and motivations which sacred symbols induce in men and the general conceptions of the order of existence which they formulate for men meet and reinforce one another.[2]

Indeed, through its rituals, Geertz contends, "the world as lived and the world as imagined, become fused under a single set of symbolic forms."[3]

Geertz is not alone in his valuation of rituals as indicators of culturally significant meanings. Jonathan Z. Smith uses the seemingly random example of leopards entering a temple, noted by both Plutarch and Kafka, to clarify the place of ritual in culture (the use of animals is coincidental to the animals in blessings addressed here). Smith presents the "dilemma" for the ritualist, and I contend a dilemma for ritual studies as well: "If everything signifies, the result will be either insanity or banality."[4] In other words, what is important enough to be ritual and what is not? Ritual, Smith contends, is "an exercise in the strategy of choice." So questions are posed: "What to include? What to hear as a message? . . . What to perceive as having double meaning?" How does one determine the "*economy of signification?*"[5]

Smith continues in this study to analyze hunting rituals and comes to the conclusion that there "appears to be a gap, an incongruity between the hunters' ideological statement of how they *ought* to hunt and their actual behavior while hunting. For me, it is far more important and interesting that they say this is the way they hunt than that they actually do so." In other words, one powerful function of ritual is to bridge the way things ought to be with the way things actually are. These gaps reveal "any society's genius and creativity."[6]

If, then, blessings of animals are increasing rapidly in numbers and in settings, does that suggest a new "world as imagined" nascent within the culture? Or, as Smith might suggest, do blessings of animals signify "a means of performing the way things ought to be in conscious tension to the way things are in such a way that this ritualized perfection is recollected in the ordinary, uncontrolled, course of things"?[7] In a society in which millions of animals are slaughtered annually for food and millions of "pets" (domesticated dogs and cats) are killed each year in municipal animal shelters (animal control facilities), do blessings of the animals offer a ritualized perfection, an idealized world? I shall return to these questions following a look at the emerging blessings of animals.

A Scattered and Brief History

> The animals of God's creation inhabit the skies, the earth, and the sea. They share in the ways of human beings. They have a part in our lives. Francis of Assisi recognized this when he called the animals, wild and tame, his brothers and sisters. Remembering Francis' love for these brothers and sisters of ours, we invoke God's blessing on these animals, and we thank God for letting us share the earth with all the creatures.[8]

Although a relatively new addition to the liturgical year for many U.S. congregations, blessings of the animals have probably taken place throughout Christian history. Though sporadic and varied in their purpose, approach, and prevalence, these blessings consistently secure a small space for animals in Christian ritual. Some evidence suggests blessings focusing on "farm" animals and the literal gift of life that they provide. But as the role of animals in human culture shifted, so did the blessings. By the early twentieth century, blessings combined thanksgivings for "pets" and for food/labor animals. As the roles of animals shifts, so do the roles of blessings—from those that acknowledge animals' usefulness to humanity, to those that also recognize their role as human companions, and to, in some cases, those that recognize their own intrinsic value.[9]

Scant evidence exists to explain the role of animal blessings over the course of the centuries. Whether included in the blessings of fields as part of rituals similar to Rogation Days or as a separate event, often associated with the Feast of St. Anthony Abbot, there is some indication that blessings are not a pure construction of the late-twentieth-century church. For example, Carola Mc-Murrough includes the following description of a blessing titled "Benedictio equorum aliorumve animalium," which took place on St. Anthony's Day in Rome in the 1930s.[10] She begins with a lengthy but fascinating description of the various categories of animals gathering for the blessing:

> On January 17th, the feast of St. Anthony of the Desert, lover and protector of animals, all the animals of Rome congregate at intervals on a sunny piazza in front of the church of St. Eusebius to receive a special blessing. . . . In the square in front of the church, in a corner of one of Rome's biggest market places, the four-footed congregation was already assembling. . . . Two lines of cab horses were already neatly drawn up, each one with the Italian colors in ribbons above his ears. . . . The humble donkeys from the adjacent market were placed behind the horses. . . . Two gaily painted wine carts form the Campagna, just about to deliver their barrels of Frascati wine, joined the assembly. Right in front, some important, beribboned pussies, in devoted mistresses' arms, Angoras and ordinary cats, scratched and spat at the great number of dogs around them. Hunting dogs, German police dogs, wire haired terriers, white woolie dogs, black curly ones, a little Roman "lupetto," all made up a right noisy and restive congregation. There were canaries in cages and other birds, and even an elephant from a passing circus. The whole assembly might have walked out of Noah's Ark onto the piazza!

Because "all the animals of Rome" congregated, one assumes that this blessing held a central place in the ritual calendar. McMurrough continues with a description of the blessing ceremony itself:

At ten o'clock, while inside the church a solemn High Mass was being celebrated in honor of the saint, a priest and acolyte in white surplices, came out on the steps; there was a hush in the congregation and some attempt made at order. The Latin prayer was read out of the ritual, very short and to the point, asking the blessing of God on these animals and that, through the intercession of St. Anthony, they might be preserved, in their bodies, from all harm, "ab omni malo." A generous sprinkling of holy water closed the brief ceremony.[11]

McMurrough describes similar rituals throughout the countryside. So, for example, in the Roman campagna a "formidable" congregation gathers as shepherds bring flocks to assigned places, often "two and three thousand head." The countryside blessings include a generous meal for the animals.[12]

Images of St. Anthony Abbot suggest that a tradition of animal blessings is connected with him, though tracing this tradition historically is difficult. One particular image dating from the early fifteenth century shows Anthony surrounded by animals and people, some of the people obviously representing the poor or the sick. Anthony faces the animals, his hand raised in blessings, as they gaze up at him. A pig, ducks, geese, a mule, sheep, and a buck stand facing him, receiving his blessing. Interestingly, the people are off to the side of the image whereas the animals are front and center. Whether this image portrays actual events is impossible to determine as no textual evidence suggests that such blessings took place. So although the possibility of continuous blessings in Italy, Germany, and other parts of Christendom is intriguing, there is no evidence that proves these blessings have taken place throughout the entire history of Christianity. Still, St. Anthony celebrations that include blessings of animals take place today in locations as distant as Rome and Mexico City, Madrid and Los Angeles.

A brief glimpse at the Olvera Street blessing in Los Angeles offers another intriguing link. The first celebration of the blessing of the animals at Olvera Street is unknown; some sources indicate 1930, whereas others date the blessing as early at the late eighteenth century.[13] The location itself, on the oldest surviving street in Los Angeles, dating from the time of Mexican rule and currently part of El Pueblo de Los Angeles Historical Monument, is historic. In the 1920s the area of downtown Los Angeles that encompasses Olvera Street was refurbished and billed as a tourist attraction, a type of "old Mexico" in the midst of the rapidly growing city. The grand opening of this central Los Angeles landscape took place in 1930, and thus that date or one shortly thereafter seems most reasonable for the beginning of this annual animal blessing.[14]

Traditionally, the blessing of the animals occurred on the Feast of San Antonio de Abad, January 17. But due primarily to weather considerations, the

Saint Anthony Abbot Blessing the Animals, the Poor, and the Sick by Master of St. Veronica. Photo courtesy of J. Paul Getty Museum.

celebration moved to Sabado de Gloria (the Saturday before Easter). March 26, 2005, marked the seventy-fifth annual celebration of the blessing. Major city officials, including the mayor of Los Angeles, attended, and the cardinal, Roger Mahony, offered the blessing, something he had done in the previous years as well. The entire event includes a procession down the central street. A cow, adorned in flowers, leads the way because, "according to tradition, she is the animal who gives most to humanity."[15] Humans provide festive costumes for the animals brought to the blessing: pugs are wrapped in ponchos, iguanas don sombreros, and tiny serapes hang on the shoulders of chihuahuas. Crowds of people gather for the event as well. In addition, a mural by Leo Politi, painted between 1974 and 1978 and part of the celebrated public art of Los Angeles, painted on the wall of the Biscailuz Building, depicts the Olvera Street blessing, thus establishing even more fully the centrality of this event for the community. The mural depicts some real figures from Olvera Street, including a tall violinist who regularly played on the streets, a woman with poodles who had a booth on the street, and even Politi's own dogs. Central to the image is a Franciscan priest blessing animals that are held up by children. The cows adorned with festive flowers are also depicted, along with myriad animals—rabbits, goats, a lamb (cradled gently in a woman's arms), dogs, and numerous birds flying through the entire scene.

This scattered history is suggestive but certainly not definitive. Blessings of animals have taken place in the history of Christianity, but they have morphed in meaning, form, and location. The concept of blessing animals, as indicated by the fifteenth-century image of St. Anthony, might be more ideal than real, even ritual-less at times. In other words, official rituals were not included in the liturgical year even though blessings of animals took place. But evidence does point to some rituals connected to St. Anthony Abbot in the early twentieth century, possibly remnants of a longer history. Regardless, the end of the twentieth century witnessed an incredible growth, or maybe a rebirth, of animal blessings as they transformed, changed, and became associated directly with the Feast of St. Francis.

Who or what is the object or the subject of these blessings is at issue, however. The category of "pet" is a recent one in the scope of human history. Animals, even domesticated ones such as the dogs, have been in the company of humans and humans in the company of animals in different ways throughout the course of history. But is a pet distinct from other animals? If so, how or why? Theologians have debated this point at times. C. S. Lewis, for example, contends that there is animal resurrection, but only for "tame animals."[16] Animals, not in themselves but "in their relation to man," enter the realm of salvation. Interestingly, it is Evelyn Underhill who counters Lewis on this assertion with a feminist gaze into and critique of his theological anthropology:

> Is the cow which we have turned into a milk machine or the hen we have turned into an egg machine really nearer the mind of God than its wild ancestor? This seems like saying that the black slave is the only natural Negro. You surely can't mean that, or think that the robin redbreast in a cage doesn't put heaven in a rage. . . . And if we ever get a sideways glimpse of the animal-in-itself, the animal existing for God's glory and pleasure and lit by His light . . . we don't owe it to the Pekinese, the Persian cat or the canary, but to some wild creature living in completeness of adjustment to Nature, a life that is utterly independent of man. . . . Of course I agree that animals too are involved in the Fall and await redemption and transfiguration. . . . And man is not doubt offered the chance of being the mediator of that redemption. But not by taming, surely? Rather by loving and reverencing the creatures enough to leave them free . . . your concept of God would be improved by just a touch of wildness.[17]

Underhill suggests that wild animals, rather than domesticated animals, provide more divine pleasure. The dominion of "man" is questioned powerfully.

Of course, the line between domesticated and wild is a blurry one. Are dogs domesticated by their choice or by human intervention or by an interaction of humans and canids at some point in history as suggested in the previous chapter? Regardless, the question of the pet or of animals in a state not as closely connected to humans is an important one. It cannot be denied that the growth of blessings is linked directly to the growth in the numbers of pets and the pet industry in the United States in the late twentieth century. Even the the names given these rituals, "Blessing of the Pets" or "Blessing of the Animals," fluctuates.

St. John the Divine and the National Cathedral

The Sunday closest to the Feast of St. Francis (October 4) marks an interesting day for animals and humans at the Cathedral of St. John the Divine in New York City.[18] Although not typical of most animal blessing liturgies studied, this one epitomizes the idea and, some might contend, the ideal of the inclusion of animals in the Christian worship setting. The liturgical event is officially titled the "Feast of St. Francis" and includes the "Holy Eucharist and Procession of Animals" presided over by the bishop of New York.[19] Barks echoing in the massive Gothic cathedral suggest that this is not the typical twenty-first-century Sunday morning Christian worship service, however.

Hopeful participants arrive as early as 7:00 A.M. to wait for the 11:00 A.M. worship service to begin because the cathedral fills to at least its thirty-five-hundred-person, standing-room-only capacity for the Feast of St. Francis ritual. Many bring animal companions with them. On one occasion, Chuckles (the parrot), Philly and Nicholae (dachshunds), and Jack the bulldog stood among humans, ferrets, cats, turtles, and numerous canines, just to name the most prominent species, in a line that spread several city blocks. Walking up and down were teenagers from the cathedral school handing out treats as they proclaimed "puppies get hungry during masses."

Upon entering the sanctuary, worshipers were enveloped by the Gothic structure, its altar ceiling high enough for the Statue of Liberty to stand (not including her pedestal).[20] Signs reading "Reserved for Large Dogs" adorned the front row of chairs in each section and a designated area for disabled humans and their service animals were next to the altar. For over an hour animals moved inside, with little or no incident, and took their places for worship. The liturgy focused on creation as a whole, and congregants learned "gestures of praise" to accompany St. Francis's "Canticle of Brother Sun" and "For the Beauty of the Earth." Several humans even worked to include their companion animals in the gesturing (with little success and to some animals' annoyance, I might add). Readings from the book of Genesis, the Psalms, the Qur'an, and the Gospel of Matthew preceded the sermon. In his homily, the dean of the cathedral, James A. Kowalski, focused on the connections between Francis's love for animals and the environment to themes of global peace, sustainability, and true security.

Powerful ancient Christian ritual elements intermingled with modern liturgical pieces. For example, the choir sang the "Kyrie" (Lord have mercy, Christ have mercy, Lord have mercy) accompanied by instrumentals interspersed with timber wolf howls and some real dog barking responses. Throughout the service, music, led by Paul Winter (known for his "Earth Mass" and "Winter Solstice Celebrations") included voices from various animals: the humpback whale joins the "Sanctus"; harp seals comprise part of the chorus for the "Agnus Dei"; and, as mentioned above, the timber wolf howls in the "Kyrie." During the actual distribution of the eucharistic elements, some people moved forward with their animal companions, participating in the eucharist together, something not unheard of in Christian history.

The final event of the formal liturgy is "The Living Earth: Opening of the Great Bronze Door and the Silent Procession." At the entrance to the sanctuary stand two massive bronze doors. According to the dean, these doors are only opened three times a year: Christmas, Easter, and the Procession of the Animals. This amazing liturgical choice suggests that the procession becomes one of the three high holy moments in the life of this congregation each year, though that designation was not officially assigned. The congregation was asked to remain silent and not to take flash photographs in order to keep the animals in the procession safe and calm. A camel, adorned with a wreath on her hump, an eagle, a beehive, two llamas, and many more animals moved into the sanctuary through the bronze doors and gathered at the altar. The congregation, both animals and human, remained astonishingly silent as the creatures walked down the center aisle. At this point, the bishop called on the entire congregation to pray together:

> We give you thanks, most gracious God, for the beauty of the earth and sky and sea; for the richness of mountains, plains, and rivers; for the songs of birds and the loveliness of flowers, and for the wonder of your animal kingdom. We praise you for these good gifts, and pray that we many safeguard them for our posterity. Grant that we may continue to grow in our grateful enjoyment of your abundant creation, to the honor and glory of your Name, now and for ever. Amen.

Following this prayer the bishop blessed all of the animals using words attributed to St. Clare: "Live without fear: your Creator loves you, made you holy, and has always protected you. Go in peace to follow the good road and may

Priests recess following the procession, Cathedral of St. John the Divine, New York. Photo by author, October 2004.

God's blessing be with you always. Amen." At the end of the formal liturgy humans and other animals moved outside for individual blessings.

Overall, although there was one slightly stressed chihuahua, the fifteen hundred or so animals (no official count is taken and the individual bees in their hive and ants in their colonies are certainly not included in this estimate) and thirty-five hundred or more people fared well during the formal, indoor liturgy.[21] An occasional growl could be heard from the tightly packed dogs, but it was amazing how silent so many animals (particularly humans) gathered in one place could be—and how loud they could be when singing along with the huge choir. As Kowalski stated, referring more specifically to the other-than-human animals, "They sense the spirit and relax. This is the way it's meant to be, together in peace and harmony."[22]

In the park outside, animals were individually blessed at four different stations. Priests placed their hands on each animal and said something similar to "Bless you now in the name of the Father, Son, and Holy Spirit; God be with you and your family now and always. Amen." After an hour, most animals present had received a blessing. In addition, food vendors (such as the Interfaith Assembly on Homeless and Housing), performers (including Josh the Juggler and the Karpathos), and pet adoption/advocacy agencies (such as Chimp Haven, Greyhound Rescue, North Shore Animal League, and Animal Care and Control of New York City) set up areas to distribute information and hope for adoptions of some of these homeless animals. Human and animal justice issues intermingle as voter registration tables, Heifer Project International, and advocates for homeless humans and animals work together.

Although a more integrative analysis is offered below, a few observations seem appropriate at this point. Animals are most definitely, and obviously, included in this major liturgical event—they are part of the Christian congregation and are invited wholeheartedly into the sanctuary. Human cultural diversity is celebrated, and the diversity of the world's species is emphasized. African dancers worship alongside traditional European, incense-bearing priests. Beehives and even algae represent the other-than-human world as fully as the prevalent canine companions. In other words, the Feast of St. Francis in this particular manifestation suggests an image of Christianity that goes well beyond the inclusion of many species; indeed, it suggests that celebrating the diversity of human culture must include the celebration of diverse species. Interconnectedness flows throughout the liturgy and the fair that follows. "The Saint Francis Celebration reaches across cultures and faiths, across ages and ideologies," said a spokesperson for the office of the dean of the cathedral. "We feel a bond in our shared responsibility under one sun, breathing the same air, drinking the waters of the earth."[23]

Blessing of a dog, Cathedral of St. John the Divine, New York. Photo by author, October 2004.

However, a certain critical assessment is necessary here. First, although the procession of animals is impressive and speaks to the centrality of animals through such actions as the opening of the bronze doors, there remains something overly idealistic and removed from reality. So, for instance, a beautiful, small cow processes into the sanctuary, yet the realities of factory farming in the United States go without mention. Many purebred dogs enter the cathedral, some of whom certainly came from rescue groups, but numerous ones also must have come from breeders; yet the city kills over twenty-eight thousand homeless dogs each year.[24] These issues are indicative of the blessing ritual as an unachieved ideal in the midst of a less-than-utopian real. One might also question whether keeping animals in a large room full of the smells of incense, shouts of human voices, and presence of thousands of other creatures for over two hours is a good experience for the animals. Then again, how would a human being ever really make that determination?

Although it has not been proven as the seminal event in the growth of blessings of the animals in the United States, one cannot deny the impact of the service at the Cathedral of St. John the Divine. This particular ritual has taken place for over twenty years now, and other congregations, after reading about the event in the newspaper or, more recently, on the Internet, decided to mirror the St. John the Divine blessing. Some would suggest that this congregation really started the trend, or at least gave impetus and energy to its growth.

Another prominent church, the National Cathedral in Washington, D.C., follows in the footsteps of its sister church in New York City, at least to a certain extent.[25] The National Cathedral celebrates the Feast of St. Francis on the actual feast day, regardless of the day of the week. The blessing of the animals takes place after the evensong. Interestingly, the cover of the bulletin for the service explains the life of St. Francis and comes to the conclusion that, although he is "one of the most popular and admired saints of Christianity," he is also "probably the least imitated." The animals in Washington gather on the front steps, not in the sanctuary, as in New York. A member of the church staff informed me that some members of the congregation do not appreciate having the animals inside the sanctuary, though the bishop does occasionally bring his dog.[26]

But the stairs leading to the main west entrance are decorated with flowers and tables prepared with symbols and implements for the blessing. Readings from the book of Genesis and from the Psalms are followed by a responsive prayer. Then three priests assume stations on the steps and invite individual animals forward for this blessing: "N. (the animal), may you be blessed in the Name of God who created you, and may you and N. (the human) enjoy life together in the name of the God who cares for you." When I observed the ritual, people and animals waited in line for their turn to be blessed, and a few, mostly animals, tried to get a drink from the holy water. As I spoke with congregants they indicated how significant this service was for them and, they sensed, for their animals. Nearly one hundred animals and humans attended, with canines as the second most prominent species (after humans). In addition to the crowd gathered for the blessing, a local group of young people who run a business providing care for dogs during the day was on hand to help, and to advertise their wares.

These two blessings at influential, large, inner-city cathedrals provide a fascinating comparison and contrast. On the one hand, numerous people (though significantly more in New York) attended the service and, in most cases, brought their animals with them. All seemed genuinely affected and expressed sincerity about their purposes at the blessings. But there were some significant differences. Whereas St. John the Divine's blessing literally opened the doors to all species, the National Cathedral maintained the distinction between humans in the sanctuary and animals on the steps. One could argue that the animals in the sanctuary were more stressed, but their

Blessing of a small animal in a crate, National Cathedral, Washington, D.C. Photo by author, October 2004.

Blessing of a dog, National Cathedral, Washington, D.C. Photo by author, October 2004.

inclusion in the sacred space marks a significant shift in the understanding of boundaries in Christianity. Then again, the space outside of the National Cathedral could also be claimed as sacred, maybe moreso than the interior space of the sanctuary.

The National Cathedral blessing is much more representative of blessings occurring across the United States. There are at least two hundred blessings taking place in forty states and the District of Columbia, and this is just a partial list.[27] In some states I have found reports of only one blessing, but in others there are as many as twenty. All evidence suggests that these numbers are dramatic underestimates.[28] A variety of denominations participate, from Catholic to Methodist to Disciples of Christ to Lutheran, Episcopalian, and Unitarian. Also interesting is the connection between secular animal organizations, such as the Humane Society, and religious communities for these events. The blessing mentioned at the beginning of this chapter, for example, was connected with the grand opening of a municipal animal shelter (thus a local government institution was sponsoring a secular-religious blessing). These historic, prominent congregations receive significantly more media coverage, but blessings throughout the United States abound.

Here, There and Everywhere in U.S. Culture

Apprehend God in all things,
For God is in all things
Every creature is full of God
If I spent enough time with the tiniest creature
Even a caterpillar
I would never have to prepare a sermon
So full of God is every creature.

This quotation, attributed to Meister Eckhart, began the message at Central Christian Church's (Dallas, Texas) Blessing of the Pets in October 2003.[29] The outline of this ritual of blessing is typical of those celebrated throughout the United States, Canada, and Australia in the early twenty-first century. It was held outdoors in the "prayer garden," included several Scripture readings and a homily, invited the congregation to join in a litany for animals, and ended with a blessing of the pets. So how are these increasingly common and, in many cases fairly standard, even across interdenominational lines, rituals practiced and understood? What does this ritual indicate about the place of animals in Christianity at this juncture in human history?

In order to gather information from a variety of Christian denominations in diverse geographical settings, I sent a survey to more than fifty churches.

The response was strong: more than thirty congregations. Initially, I posed these questions: How many people and animals are present for the event? What animals are present? Why did your congregation decide to hold this event? In your opinion, does it have particular meaning for certain groups in the congregation or community? Has anyone ever "complained" about it? How do you understand it to fit within Christianity? How many times have you held this event and do you plan on continuing it? In addition, I requested a copy of the liturgy, and most of the responding congregations included this information. A variety of images of the blessings and a list of websites about blessings were generated from the research. In order to identify trends, I compared the responses to the basic questions posed, then analyzed liturgies, noting similarities and differences. With this information, along with numerous research visits to blessings of the pets over several years, I propose an initial interpretation of this rapidly growing liturgical phenomenon in the United States.

The size and membership (species) of the congregations (human and animal) gathered varied, from around twenty to over five thousand participants. Also, a percentage of the blessing events connected to local animal rescue and adoption events, thus shifting the dynamic in interesting ways. In general, however, there are by far more dogs and humans present than other species. But as Father Carpenter in Mesa, Arizona, stated, "I've also blessed cats, birds, hamsters, gerbils, mice, rats, lizards, snakes, and the occasional rabbit." Some humans bring the ashes of deceased pets to have them blessed postmortem.[30] The blessings also appeared to attract different crowds, in addition to the diverse species. So at a Presbyterian church in California, about one hundred humans were there, and "interestingly enough, this is better attended by the community at large rather than just members of the congregation."[31]

Another question raised in the area of attendance at these events is the inclusion of animals for display or educational purposes. At Shepherd of the Desert Lutheran Church, located in the Mojave Desert, a "biologist from the local Army base has a display of live desert animals . . . that he takes around to schools. He was there with his collection of live spiders, scorpions, snakes, an owl, and a hawk." At St. John the Divine, part of the festival following the blessing offered a petting zoo and, indeed, though astounding and beautiful for human spectators, the procession of animals that included a camel, a hedgehog, a reindeer, and myriad other species might bring a problematic aspect to this ceremony.

When asked why they hold blessings events, respondents gave a variety of answers. Some focused specifically on the animals present and their roles, others on the humans present and their responsibilities. For example, St. Paul's Anglican Church (Manuka, Australia, the only congregation outside of the United States included in this research) "draws attention to the broad context of our life in God's creation, and honours the role of our pets." Whereas at Central Christian Church in Dallas, it was offered as a way to provide "outreach to those who might not otherwise attend church"; in other words, it was part of an evangelism program for humans. Other congregations suggested several reasons. San Ramon Valley United Methodist Church in California holds the blessings for three reasons: "One, to honor the place of animals in our lives and as a way to recognize and respect all of creation (the St. Francis tie-in). Second, it was a way to publicize the Heifer Project. Thirdly, we hoped it would be an outreach to the larger community, attracting non-church goers from our surrounding community." Another respondent mentioned the importance of how God's creatures "minister to us."[32]

The question of whether the blessings of pets/animals has a particular meaning for participants drew rather short, and in general vague, answers. This list of responses captures the overall sense of the "meaning" question:

> "It tells the pet lovers that we care and even prayers for their pets are important"; "It does not seem to have deep significance"; "Yes, for those who believe that animals and pets are truly a gift from God"; "Initially we thought children might enjoy it, and they do; but I think older people enjoy it too. Pets play a pivotal role in the lives of older adults, especially those who live alone"; "I think people like the idea that their beloved pets are an intentional and significant part of God's creation."

The range was rather dramatic—from not having "deep significance" to "what greater lesson for us is there?" Obviously, this is a ritual whose meaning is not only contested but also changing rapidly.

Another aspect of this contestation of meaning came out in responses to the question "Has anyone ever 'complained' about it?" The vast majority of respondents indicated that nobody has ever complained, though some might not fully understand the purpose of the blessing. Others were more emphatic about the blessings' approval rating: "How could you complain about the blessing of animals???!!!" Still, questions arose. At one congregation a member of the pastoral staff "thought it was kind of silly—the 'care for the poor not the poodles' perspective." Another respondent noted, "One lady will not come." All of the congregations that responded indicated that they were planning on continuing the blessing of the animals in the years to come, and several suggested they would be expanding the event.

How, then, does this ritual fit within Christianity? As the survey was put together, this question seemed to be the most complex, but the answers it elicited point to a ritual that has not yet developed an in-depth theology surrounding it. In other words, answers were particularly simplistic in most cases. Still, a few trends became apparent. First, the broader creation or environmental aspect seemed integral because animals or pets serve as reminders that we "are part of God's creation." They "draw us more deeply into the larger circle of life, into the wonder of our common relationship with our Creator." Second, a theological anthropology, though never named as such, came through clearly. Animals are "not only creations of God but blessings as well." In other words, they have value and should be blessed because of their service to humanity and, according to many Christians, our requisite role and biblical mandate of stewardship: "God created the animals and the rest of nature and commissioned us humans to be stewards of creation. That implies loving animals. This event was a way to demonstrate that love." Humans receive animals as "a gift from God" and have "responsibilities" toward them; the blessings reinforce that idea of human stewardship over animals. Rather than existing for themselves, "God gives us these wonderful animal companions as another way to show us his unconditional love for us." The theme of human as steward comes through clearly in one of the most complete responses received:

> I think all of creation belongs to God as we are obligated to care for it. Since we are Christians, we don't worship the sun or the sky or the birds. We expand and deepen our worship of the Creator when we feel responsible for protecting God's handiwork. The idea that humanity is to be a steward of the Earth and its inhabitants acknowledges the intricate web that binds all life together. I also think it is an aspect of pastoral care when we acknowledge the role animals, especially companion animals, increasingly play in our urban/suburban lives. In more agrarian times, people asked God's blessings for their work animals and livestock. I can't imagine that pastors back then ever wondered if it was the right thing to do. To bless pets is a way for us to interact and care for our congregation—to demonstrate that we care about the things they care about!

Animals in these blessings function as reminders of human's role as steward, of animals as servants, divinely ordained by God to work for humanity, as companions for people who, as urban dwellers, increasingly find themselves one step removed from nature.

Reminiscent of the theories of Geertz and Smith, some respondents pointed to the ideal world yet to be achieved, though the ritual of blessing strives toward this new Eden. The blessing of animals "reminds us of God's new creation, where the lamb will lie down with the lion." Animals point to the "unconditional love" of God, a symbol or an indicator of the divine. Pets "represent the purest love" because they "don't care what we look like, how we act towards them, or what we do for a living." In the midst of this idealization of pets, this disconnect between pets and food animals, an ideal world of unconditional love was performed.

It was also telling that one response to the question of meaning was a question mark: "?" Certainly a broad understanding of recognizing animals as companions, as objects of our stewardship or representatives of God's love, wove throughout the reflections on meaning. But as a whole the responses were particularly unresponsive. Many question marks remain in the minds of those who enact blessings of animals. The ritual might still be, in its own way, a bit of a mystery.

The final aspect of this phase of research that rose to the surface is the interfaith and religious-secular nature of blessings. Obviously the blessings at St. John the Divine—with readings from the Qur'an, liturgical dancers from Africa, and, arguably, symbols of pagan or nature-based traditions marking the entire service—reflect the interfaith and intercultural aspects of the ritual. But the interfaith and extrafaith traits extend beyond this already ecumenical congregation. For example, King of Peace Episcopal Church participates in more than one blessing of the pets each year, both in early October. As part of the "Rock Shrimp Festival," they join with a Catholic church and another Episcopal church for a blessing that is sponsored by Friends of Greyhounds, a ritual both ecumenical and religious-secular. The next weekend they join with the Humane Society for a blessing of the pets at that location. This congregation moves out of its traditional worship space and goes elsewhere for the blessing of the pets, but does so more than once and joins with secular animal organizations for the worship rituals.[33]

In Long Beach, California, the Haute Dog organization sponsors an even more inclusive blessing of animals that blurs the lines between secular and religious. As part of the Friends of Long Beach Animal Appreciation Day, the blessing was one of several events, including 2K/5K Walk for the Animals. More than two hundred people, along with their "penitent pets," attended the blessing. A Catholic priest, the minister of the local United Church of Religious Science, the lead pastor of the nondenominational Springs of Life Fellowship, and a clergyperson ordained by the Universal Life Church presided together. The organization's website described the pet blessing ceremony as "the first interfaith type in the region."[34]

Blessings of the pets/animals take place in Christian communities all over the world, not just in the United States. The *Manila Times* reports on a Philippine animal welfare society's Animal Blessing Day, which takes place at the

Mary the Queen Parish and Mt. Carmel Church on the Saturday or Sunday closest to October 4 every year.[35] St. Mary's School in St. Croix in the Virgin Islands, along with the St. Croix Animal Shelter, holds an event each year.[36] Doing viable research into the global Christian phenomenon proved beyond the capacity of this particular study, however, and thus I included only one international congregation in the information above, but it is certainly an area that warrants further attention.

A Blessing or a Circus Display

Although a blessing of the pets/animals becomes a new ritual moment in many Christian congregations and such a ritual invites animals to be part of the Christian community for at least 1 of the 365 days each year, does it simply reimpose the animal as a subject of the dominator's gaze? And as ritual theory is applied to a study of these blessings, is the tension between the actual and the ideal realities so stark in blessings of the pets that they fail to effectively address "fundamental conflicts and contradictions in the society," arguably a central aspect of ritual?[37] I think both could be the case.

Berger concludes his essay "About Looking" with a description of zoos, which, he contends, marginalize animals completely. They spend their lives in a less-than-real world where they can be "seen, observed, studied." In a zoo, "[h]owever you look at these animals," even when they are close to you, "you are looking at something that has been rendered absolutely marginal."[38] Do the blessings also, in their very invitation to animals at only this one time and for only this one purpose, also render animals absolutely marginal? Blessings of pets/animals seem to fit the mold of other displays:

> Zoos, realistic animal toys and the widespread commercial diffusion of animal imagery, all began as animals started to be withdrawn from daily life. One could suppose that such innovations were compensatory. Yet in reality the innovations themselves belonged to the same remorseless movement as was dispersing the animals. The zoos, with their theatrical décor for display, were in fact demonstrations of how animals had been rendered absolutely marginal. The realistic toys increased the demand for the new animal puppet: the urban pet. . . . Everywhere animals disappear.[39]

Blessings of the pets return animals to the sanctuary, maybe, or at least to the stairs leading to the doors of the sanctuary, but as a display and only for a few moments. Then, for another year, the space closes again and only the human approaches the altar. Some have even called blessings "the sanctuary sideshow" or a "dog and pony show."[40] Do blessings place animals in the gaze of the "arrogant eye," a term used by Marilyn Frye in her feminist critique of the gaze of patriarchy? She contends that arrogant eyes organize "everything seen with reference to themselves and their own interests."[41] Are blessings of animals mere spectator sports with the animals as objects subject to our dominating gaze?

From this research it seems that such is sometimes the case. For example, when congregations hold these events with the primary purpose of increasing their human membership—blessings of animals as a tool for evangelism— then, indeed, animals are subjects caught in the agenda of humans with a solely human-related outcome. And although the spectacle is fabulous and the outcome is a mixture, the St. John the Divine media event each October hints at an alternative purpose, one more focused on human ends than on the well-being of the animals who are blessed. As the small cow walked precariously and fearfully down the front steps of the cathedral following the blessing, her presence there seemed more coerced than genuine.

But is there only one way of looking? Might multiple ways of looking take place simultaneously in the participants and observers? In "Seeing, Looking, Watching, Observing Nonhuman Animals," Garry Marvin engages Berger's question ("Why look at animals?") and posits different ways of looking. "Watching" and "observing," for example, entail more than a passive glance or an "arrogant eye." Observing is "concentrated, attentive," and watching "indicates that time is being given to the process; one does not watch in a moment."[42] Frye also suggests alternative ways of looking. The "loving eye does not make the object of perception into something edible, does not try to assimilate it, does not reduce it to the size of the seer's desire, fear, and imagination."[43] Blessing of the animals might provide a venue for a change of the eye from arrogant to loving, or at least a step in that direction. In his critical analysis of zoos and their role in the way Western humans view animals, Ralph Acampora states that "such a transformation is palpable . . . changing over from the vision of arrogance to that of love could produce remarkably beneficial results . . . for interspecies relationships."[44]

Blessings of animals incorporate humans and other animal species into a ritual together, and this is deeply significant. Remember that although their significance is contested, rituals can be considered as "consecrated behavior." They are not taken lightly, even when embedded into a culture to an extent that they are no longer noticed. And formal religious rituals provide occasions for signifying that which matters most to a society. So animals in these blessings are participants, though, granted, rather passive participants because they probably did not choose the activity, but they are "blessed," and that is not insignificant. At least for the humans who bring their animal companions to these rituals, there is meaning. As Jack Wintz observed about a blessing over which he officiated, "It was wonderful to see the caring, reverent attitude that people displayed toward their animals. I felt a special bond with these creatures as they moved, rather amazingly, from frenzied yelping and snarling to peaceful serenity as the blessing proceeded."[45]

Additional questions are posed regarding the nature of blessings by participants or by those who refuse to participate, and sometimes these questions get to the heart of the internal struggle regarding the place of animals in Christianity and the role of this ritual in the tradition. James Kowalski, dean of the Cathedral of St. John the Divine, noted that "some say it is pagan, or not religious, or not Christian enough," though he indicated that "few attend and leave with that impression."[46] Some people refuse to be involved with animals in the Christian tradition based on their own understanding of the religion's focus on the human-God relationship. The ambiguous location of animals in Christianity bursts forth in early October!

So what might be the impetus driving this animal blessing phenomenon in U.S. Christianity? Animals occupy a tenuous place in the early twenty-first century. There are more pets, or domesticated animals, living in households with humans and serving primarily as companions in the United States than at any other time in history. As a matter of fact, the increase in the numbers of pets has been dramatic. In 2004 there were over seventy-eight million cats and sixty-five million dogs, to name the two most prominent species, living as family pets in the United States.[47] In terms of household percentages, in 1988, 56 percent of U.S. households included a pet; in 2004, 63 percent did.[48] All indications point to a continuation of this trend. It might even be more significant that the pet "industry" is growing almost exponentially, doubling between 1994 and 2004.[49] Thus there are significant numbers of pets and they are becoming increasingly visible via the media and marketing industry in the United States. Blessing them might be a wise marketing strategy for churches, as indicated by the number of responses about blessings and their connection to evangelism or church growth.

But although the growth in the numbers and market power of pets increases, so do the numbers of other animals—pigs, chickens, cows—that exist as commodities and not as the creatures so loved by God who serve as the focal point of the animal blessings. In 2003, although more than 140 million animals lived as pets, almost 10 billion were slaughtered as part of the growing farm factory industry. According to a World Farm Animals Day 2004 press release, the "average American is directly responsible for the abuse and death of 2,485 chickens, 78 turkeys and ducks, 33 pigs, and 11 cows and sheep during a 75-year life span."[50] Interestingly, World Farm

Animals Day, an event that has been sponsored for more than twenty-two years by various animal rights–related and public interest organizations, including FARM (Farm Animal Reform Movement), is recognized annually on October 2, the birthday of Mahatma Gandhi, two days prior to the Feast of St. Francis. These two events, the blessing of animals and the recognition of farm animals, mark the strained ambiguity of these creatures.

Ritual as image of the ideal in the midst of the starkness of the real—this ambiguity marks the blessings of animals. They seem to portray a culture in tension, stuck between loving animal companions and suffering animal servants. We look at animals as objects yet cradle them in our arms as precious subjects approaching the priest for a blessing. After the blessing ritual, many return to the secular world to consume the suffering of other animals, the ones not present in front of the altar or gathered on the steps approaching the bronze doors of the cathedral. Certainly blessings of animals offer possibilities for a place at the table of Christianity, but they are not yet confronting the reality. Secure in their brief ideal world, these rituals provide participants with a sense of what might be but leave them comfortable with what is.

7. Animals Are Good to Think

Transforming Theological Considerations of Animals

Shifts of consciousness, sometimes gradual, sometimes dramatic, are not beyond the wit of the human species. What is significant is that sometimes dream-like, visionary hypotheses suddenly acquire a powerful hold on the collective imagination and release new bursts of moral energy. The divine right of humans may be an idea whose time has gone. That humans should use their power in defence of the weak, especially the weak of other species, and that humans should actively seek the liberation of all beings capable of knowing their oppression and suffering may be an idea who times has come.[1]

Christianity, in its orthodox and primarily patriarchal structure, takes no real account of other-than-human animals, even when the many peripheral accounts included in the first six chapters of this book are considered. This lack of accounting for animals holds true for the first legalized forms of Christianity in the fourth century to its many variably official forms in the twenty-first century, be they evangelical U.S. or traditional Catholic orthodox, or any other of the many shapes the religion takes. Historically, the major theological works of such figures as Thomas Aquinas, John Calvin, and Karl Barth, the central doctrines and creeds of the both the Roman Catholic and Orthodox churches, and the primary themes of the Protestant world focus on human beings and the human relationship with the divine. Humans are of ultimate concern, with little or no regard for other animals. The culmination of the anthropocentric model in constructive theology and philosophy, as well as anthropocentric scriptural exegesis, melded with the philosophy of the Enlightenment to conclude that a fundamental and divinely ordained difference exists between humans and animals. As Karl Barth posits in *Church Dogmatics*, "God's eternal Son and Logos did not will to be an angel or animal but man," and "this and this alone was the content of the eternal divine election of grace."[2]

Overall, Christian theological consideration of animals meant either dismissing them altogether or using them as a stepladder to reach humanity, poised as a species at the apex of creation and in unique relationship with God. "Dumb animals and plants are devoid of the life of reason . . . they are naturally enslaved and accommodated to the uses of others," states Aquinas.[3] Though slightly more complex, as noted early, animals hold the same place in the hierarchy of John Calvin, who, in his commentary on Genesis, states explicitly that "man" should "have authority over all living creatures" because God "expressly subjects the animals to him."[4] Other theologians throughout Christian history mirror these ideas, though an occasional aberration does break into the dialogue. But although not creating a chasm greater than it is, the lives of saints-mystics, with their various connections to animals, and the ideas of theologians, with their dismissal of animals, mark the extremities of the other-than-human in Christian history, life, and thought.

And, indeed, when one delves into theological anthropology, particularly as it builds on the figure of Jesus, the gap widens. As Andrew Linzey explains:

> The incarnation is used as the trump card to vanquish all other creaturely rights to specialness, intrinsic worth, and respectful treatment. And once perceived as central—as the doctrine of incarnation surely is—all other doctrines are then reinforced from this centre. The result is a narrowing of theological focus. Contrary to the biblical evidence, the notion of covenant is applied solely to human subjects. Atonement doctrine specifically, if not exclusively, concerns humanity's redemption. The work of the creative Spirit is telescoped into the salvation of human souls. And creation is seen only as the background or theatre to the real work of God performed for, on behalf of, the divinely elected human species which is now viewed as God's exclusive concern.[5]

Theologies emphasizing God's incarnation as a human (and as a male human) combined with cultural ideologies developed during the Enlightenment, particularly humanism and its focus on the individual, transformed animals into mere objects. No longer worthy of the attention of the divine and certainly not inherently worthy in their own being, animals became tools for human use and disappeared from religious dialogue.

So what happened? How did the granted image disappear from Christian art, story, narrative, drama, and ritual? Why did the saints stop attaching themselves to animals, saving them from hunters, and providing them with fresh water in return for companionship and care? What made the blessings cease (prior to their still questionable reappearance in the late twentieth century)? I turn now to a brief overview of the demise of animals, specifically addressing issues related to the Enlightenment. With the demise in mind, I suggest that in some ways a resurrection of animals occurs in contemporary theological dialogue through such voices as Jay Mcdaniel, Stephen Webb, Sallie Mcfague, Andrew Linzey, and Matthew Scully. Although their ideas vary significantly and are even in tension with one another at times, they all share a focus on animals as valid subjects of Christian theology. As will be seen below, however, the position of animals in their theological constructs differs dramatically, and I use a feminist approach to question some of these ideas. This analysis of their theological concerns, combined with an examination of the possibilities latent in blessings of animals and the growth of ecologically conscious Christianity, suggests the potential return of animals to the Christian sanctuary.

The Demise of the Animal in Christianity

> Sticks and Stones May Break My Bones,
> But Words Can Really Hurt Me[6]

> For after the error of those who deny God, which I believe I have
> already adequately refuted, there is none that leads weak minds
> further from the straight path of virtue than that of imagining that
> the souls of the beasts are of the same nature as ours.[7]

Following his exposition on animals as inferior based on their lack of human language, Descartes draws the above-quoted conclusion, that it is a great error and a failing of weak minds to imagine that the souls of beasts are of the same nature as those of humans. For Descartes, this determination is finally proven through the difference in language. As I have already quoted Bacon's *New Atlantis* and Descartes' *Discourse on Method* at length (in chapter 2), it is not necessary to revisit those humanocentric ideological positions; the confluence of their ideas regarding the use of "words" with those of the Protestant Reformation are striking. Therefore, I focus briefly at this point on the demise of animals based on the elevation of human language, with all the far-reaching implications of its impact.

The complex of society that accompanied Descartes' pronouncement removed animals from almost any realm of the sacred. Central is the combination with the new Protestant religious ethos emerging from the sixteenth-century Reformation. To a large extent, the Reformation marked the demise of animals as saints disappeared, as people removed iconography from the sanctuary, and as a new focus centered on the spoken Word (preaching) as the only true source of revelation. All of this dominated the Protestant religious worldview. The Word meant that, once and for all, other-than-human animals, who neither speak with a human voice nor read texts, cannot carve out a spot in the Christian system.

When Martin Luther officially began the process of dismantling unified Christianity in Europe, though the unity was always something of a misperception, one of the central tenets of the newly formed Protestant communions was an elevation of the Word over the other sacraments of the church. Indeed, over the course of the Reformation in its various forms, all but two of the sacraments (baptism and the eucharist, and possibly penance in Luther's system) were scrapped altogether as formal sacraments by the majority of Protestant denominations; the other five—confirmation, penance and reconciliation, holy orders, matrimony, and anointing of the sick—might remain but with a dramatically decreased significance, or they might remain only in certain manifestations of Protestantism (for example, anointing of the sick still forms a major component, albeit in a different form, in Pentecostal Christianity). Here it should be noted that baptism and the Eucharist are two of the sacraments most likely to include animals—interesting to say the least. But the Word certainly does not include animals; as a matter of fact, it excludes them more fully than any other aspect of Christian life. Certainly a few saints thought animals could hear the Word. St. Francis preached to the birds and they responded; St. Anthony's sermon to the fish is well known. Still, the Word changed with the advent of the Reformation, becoming much more human-focused than ever before.

When Luther and Calvin refer to the "Word of God," they meant more than human speech, of course, and certainly more than preaching. They understood the Word of God to be the active creating agent that morphed into human form in the figure of Jesus. In the church, though, the Word of God took the form of preaching, and this was of ultimate significance. As Luther stated in his 1522 publication *Church Postil,* "Christ did not command the apostles to write, but only to preach."[8] Calvin seems to echo this elevation of preaching: "In short, why is the preaching of the gospel so often styled the kingdom of God, but because it is the scepter by which the heavenly King rules his people?"[9]

This focus on the Word combined with an emphasis on the salvation of the individual to help create an easy melding between humanism and the emergent Protestant worldview. I won't delve into individualism at this point, but the confluence of this new focus on individual salvation with the humanism and emphasis on language of rights hailing from the Enlightenment made for yet another leap away from animals and from nature as a whole. As Paul Santmire contends in his ecological history of Christianity, "Rising above nature in order to enter into communion with God became a hallmark of Protestant thought."[10]

Language continued its meteoric rise in philosophical and religious life throughout the eighteenth, nineteenth, and twentieth centuries. As humans and their particular abilities for communication through metaphorical and abstract concepts, and through written texts, became even more central to religious life, the demise of animals was assured. But the late twentieth and early twenty-first centuries witnessed a return of animals to Christian theological and philosophical inquiry, though from quite different directions. I turn to several of these theological constructs at this point, then ask where they seem to be taking the tradition.

God, Dogs, and Dominion

> [T]he best way to imagine how God loves the animals
> is to look at how people love pets.[11]

It seems that the great chain of being remains central to many Christian theological systems, even those that purport to take animals seriously. Stephen Webb and Matthew Scully offer two such theological constructs to the animal rights and religion dialogue. In both cases the authors present significant and telling material criticizing the current state of animals in U.S. culture. Both deplore industrialized factory farming, point to the violence of hunting for sport, and recognize the tenuous position that companion animals hold. In so doing, they give an audience that might not otherwise approach issues of animal suffering an entry point, and that is indeed significant. But at what price is this door opened?

In *On God and Dogs: A Christian Theology of Compassion for Animals,* Stephen Webb approaches animals through a "theology of excess," beginning with the concept of the "pet," specifically the pet dog. "How do we widen the closed circle of the family dog (an honorary human being) to the infinite circle of the family of all living beings?" he asks.[12] Webb's theology of animals is ultimately centered on the human-God relationship, but it takes into account the animal "other," a concept that he problematizes through the sentimentality of pet keeping. He also writes "for two different audiences, groups that ordinarily do not read the same books: people who are interested in animal rights and people who study Christian theology."[13] It is an interesting statement and one that identifies, immediately, that the author is aware of his own need to tread lightly and remain within a certain comfort zone for particular people who study Christian theology (and maybe particular people who are interested in animal rights).

The center of his theory seems to emerge in his discussion of "reading excess" or "hyperbole incarnate." After describing several different approaches to language and animals, including those of Vicki Hearne and Ursula LeGuin, Webb moves to "dog stories," which, he concludes, if "true to their subject, cannot be anything but extravagant."[14] So the best dog and animal stories "are the ones that embrace the oddness, the exuberance, the poetry of pet relationships, and thus empower the reconceptualization of the human-animal relation that conceptuality itself cannot achieve."[15] This different way of expressing relationship with pets leads to Webb's "rule of hyperbole." If the human-dog relationship, properly understood in its excess and expressed as such, can "empower our lives with an outward emanating care," then this will "hyperbolize our relationships with others." He connects this to Martin Buber's *I and Thou* ideas at this point. Buber points to the "eyes of an animal," which have "the capacity of great language," so that when ones looks into the eyes of an animal the animal looks back and asks, "Do I concern you?"[16]

Webb's "theology and dogtalk" follows this exploration into the hyperbolic. Here, I think, in the midst of this potentially powerful theology lies its potentially powerful weakness. He begins by stating that the "interconnections among God, humans, and dogs are rich." Indeed, his exposition up to this point examines these rich ties, particularly in terms of otherness, language, and relationships. But then God and dogs become too intermingled, too much of a projection, as a result of humanity taking center stage:

> Both God and dogs love unconditionally, both God and humans are masters in their own realms, and both dogs and humans are creatures and servants. Humans are in between, both masters and servants, loved by God and dogs alike. God's venture across a great divide to identify with humanity is not unlike the humans project of domesticating and adopting the canine species. Moreover, dogs, like God, are both infinitely close to us and mysteriously far away, everyday and unfathomable, immanent and transcendent.[17]

The human is the center, the link between the divine and the rest of creation, classic, Thomistic theological anthropology writ large.

Webb does not end the discussion here; the cosmic Christ emerges in his closing passages. He claims that "the incarnation has relevance for animals," answering Linzey's above-quoted critique about Christianity's central claims of incarnation as the epitome of anthropocentrism, though Webb knows some will call this "sacrilegious blasphemy."[18] Based on the eschatological and cosmic Christ, not yet fully revealed, this message of Christianity, Webb contends, "extends outward and equalizes relationships . . . so that all animals are brought into the human family, not as equals but as dependents whose needs are worthy of respect."[19]

Themes of dependence mark the work of Matthew Scully as well. Scully, an unlikely thinker on these matters, entered the dialogue about animals and Christianity with his book *Dominion: The Power of Man, the Suffering of Animals, and the Call to Mercy*. Senior speechwriter and assistant to President George W. Bush for over a year, he does not classify himself as a theologian and self-identifies as a "conservative," an "unlikely friend to the animal advocates."[20] But from the beginning his book examines humanity's relationship with animals from a Christian perspective and provides a strong critique of dominant culture's use of animals. Each chapter opens with either verses from the Bible or a quotation from a Christian theologian or mystic, such as Augustine or Basil. With this framework of religious dominion in mind, Scully confronts the major contemporary issues for human-animal interaction in the Western world: factory farming, the hunting of exotic animals for sport, whaling, and animal intelligence. He also takes on myriad philosophical positions that address animals, such as those of Peter Singer, claiming that he does not "need some utilitarian philosopher to do the moral math" for him or a "contractualist philosopher to define for me an 'appropriate object of sympathy'" or "behavioral scientists or cognitive theorists to distinguish which pains are 'real' pains and which are not." Rather, he contends, there are "moments when you do not need doctrines, when even rights become irrelevant, when life demands some basic response of fellow-feeling and mercy and love."[21]

Central to Scully's thesis is the concept that humans have power over animals and that, therefore, rights language and the concept of equality will not solve the issue of animal suffering. A hierarchy exists in his theological consideration of animals because humans "love animals as only the higher love the lower, the knowing love the innocent, and the strong love the vulnerable."[22] For him, the traditional biblical language of "dominion" proves central; as a matter of fact, his book opens with Genesis 1:24–26, using the translation "let them have dominion over" as God's word to humans. Scully defines how dominion plays out in the contemporary relationships of humans and animals:

> Animals are more than ever a test of our character, of mankind's capacity for empathy and for decent, honorable conduct and faithful stewardship. We are called to treat them with kindness, not because they have rights or power or some claim to equality, but in a sense because they don't; because they all stand unequal and powerless before us. Animals are so easily overlooked, their interests so easily brushed aside. Whenever we humans enter their world, from our farms to the local animal shelter to the African savanna, we enter as lords of the earth bearing strange powers of terror and mercy alike.[23]

As "lord of the earth," human dominion acts itself out through "terror and mercy."

With graphic details and powerful imagery Scully displays the dominion of humanity, reinforcing his contention that this power cannot be denied. For example, in "The Shooting Field," one of his book's chapters, he describes the annual convention of the Safari Club International (SCI), which he attended in 1999. From keynote speaker General Schwarzkopf to former president George H. W. Bush to South Dakota governor Joe Foss, Scully lists the powerful and influential members of this hunting society. Then he turns to the Christian Sportsmen's Fellowship, with its motto "On Target to Catch Men for Christ."[24] Here the main speaker reminds those gathered that "SCI is so important, because it protects our right to hunt," then follows that statement with a reminder that if "you have the Lord on your side, you'll win." In order not to lose the connection, he follows this with "I believe in the Bible and everything in it. Every one of you is a miracle. Every human being is a miracle. It's hard to believe—there are so many of us—but it's true. Think about it. A miracle, the world created for you. You're it."[25] This anthropocentrism is perfectly in line with the Safari Club's "Crowning Achievement Award," a "coveted honor" recognizing individuals who have "extinguished the minimum-required 322 animals."[26]

In his analysis of SCI, Scully draws the direct links between this ideology of hunting and biblical concepts of dominion: "That is what the Bible says, and that is what the folks at Safari Club think they are doing: the relentless, rewarding, natural, and praiseworthy work of dominion. Quite literally, as we saw at the SCI prayer breakfast, not a one of them is burdened by the least doubt that they are bringing God's will to nature, with every shot proclaiming His glory. Go hunting . . . and it's tough to go wrong."[27] Of course, Scully's interpretation of these same biblical injunctions is quite different from that of SCI, though he finally seems to decide that "citing the Bible chapter and verse doesn't prove much except that fallen man has once again made a mess of things."[28]

Just as it critiques the hunting ideology of SCI, *Dominion* critiques the food production system of the United States, which has led to industrial animal farming. After visiting a factory farm and seeing the housing for pigs there, Scully asks, "How does a man rest at night knowing that in this strawless dungeon of pens are all of these living creatures under his care, never leaving except to die, hardly able to turn or life down, horror-stricken by every opening of the door, biting and fighting and going mad[?]"[29]

With these and other contemporary animal-human interactions in mind, Scully argues that mercy, rather than rights, is the concept most likely to change human relationships with suffering animals:

This credo in its way is far more subversive than anything to be found in the manifestos of environmentalism or animal rights, for it asks not only to conserve and manage and protect the creatures, but to reserve a little bit of love for them too. When a man slays an elephant, or ensnares a wolf in his leg-hold traps, or loads his livestock in and out of trucks as if hauling trash, to call him merciless is a far graver accusation than to call him a violator of rights or squandered of natural resources. He will take far greater offense at the charge, and he should.[30]

Pragmatic as well as theological reasoning underlies his conclusions. After examining the various arbitrary and inconsistent laws passed to ensure certain rights to animals, and upon admitting that animals do have the capacity to suffer, he discards the possibility of agreement on the basic "rights" societies should grant to animals: "With animals we accept no such claims of absolute value, and so are left without any common and consistent standard. Ultimately, in the weighing of goods and interests, there's nothing on their side of the scale to counterbalance our demands upon them." But the "logic of our own laws" confronts us when some animals are classified as property, others as food, and still others as objects of sport.[31]

So, he concludes, "[a]ll that animals need, and what we owe them under our laws, are specific, clear, and above all consistent criminal sanctions declaring Thou Shalt Not subject them to human cruelty, as a matter of simple decency and an obligation of justice." Then, while Scully leaves the spiritual questions for each individual to ponder, he states his position that the "spectators and participants who delight in cruelty to animals . . . can worry about their own souls."[32] Ultimately, the concept of dominion, as drawn from Genesis and from the entire sweep of Christian tradition, lead to the conclusion that "in every act of kindness we hold in our own hands the mercy of our Maker, whose purposes are in life and not death."[33]

In the foreword to Webb's *On God and Dogs* Andrew Linzey states that Webb's thesis "will not be music to the ears of all his fellow travelers—and I am one of them."[34] I join Linzey. The thesis is not music to my ears, either. Scully and Webb strike a note of patriarchal conservatism, the same theologies of animals that have been integral to dominant Christianity for years, only with a touch of hate at twenty-first century capitalism's particular use of this hierarchy. So raging at the machine that leads to industrial farming and animals as mass commodity has the potential to raise awareness of animal suffering (the same machine that turns humans into mass commodities as well). But if animals remain utterly subordinate to the power of humans, what has changed as a result of this rage? In her essay "Of Mice and Men," Catharine MacKinnon, addressing the treatment of women and animals, notes that the "denial of social hierarchy in both relations is further supported by verbiage about love and protection. . . . The idea is, love of men for women or people for animals, motivating their supposed protection, mitigates the domination."[35] If animal-aware theologies dismiss animal rights in favor of mercy (dominion) and compassion (pets), the hierarchical structures that allow for the exploitation of animals based on human superiority have not changed. Again, MacKinnon puts it clearly after analyzing Steinbeck's *Of Mice and Men:* "The good intentions of the powerful, far from saving the powerless, doom them. Unless you change the structure of the power system you exercise, that you mean well may not save those you love. Animal rights advocates take note."[36] Certainly "animal rights" has layers of problems associated with it, as Peter Singer and Andrew Linzey have so articulately explained. But to replace even the possibility with dominion and pets seems absurd.

Furthermore, mercy and pet keeping, even when they are enacted by some slices of society, are less than ideal. A dog rescue group posts this poem to remind people that only a small percentage of so-called pets experiences fulfilling lives:

> I ask for the privilege of not being born . . .
> not to be born until you can assure me of a home,
> and the right to live as long as I am physically able to enjoy life . . .
> not be born until my body is precious and people have
> ceased to exploit it because it is cheap and plentiful.[37]

So a theological system that idealizes a relationship (human-pet) that is so often deeply troubled and violent, for pets, seems problematic indeed.

To have pets, to address animals from a position of sheer power that is maintained by assuming a response only valid from that position, mitigates the issue momentarily but fails to recognize animals as intrinsically worthy. The trap into which Webb and Scully fall here is the same one of Aquinas, Barth, and Calvin—defining other animals by humanity's unique relationship to God and humanity's superiority over animals. Indeed, it may not be a trap at all, but a guise to continue the authoritarian system that has held sway over human culture and all of the other species it touches for millennia. Inherently patriarchal theological and cultural ideologies simply cannot respond to the crisis of animals at this point in history.

Theocentrism, Panentheism, and the Body of God

Determining which theologians to address in this section was more difficult than initially imagined, indicative of the shift in theological consideration of animals. While there are still too few such pieces in place, at least the idea of animals as a subject of Christian theological speculation is no longer seen as outside the realm of possibility. The three theologians presented here—Andrew Linzey, Jay McDaniel, and Sallie McFague—fall on a kind of continuum from more traditional, orthodox to more radical, ecofeminist positions. As a matter of fact, within individual systems these positions sometimes blur. But in each case they are taking animals seriously as animals, not only in relationship to humans, though, again, that is the only position they (or we) can truly inhabit. Attempts are made to rethink animals in ways that move animals into their own spheres and outside that dominated by humanity.

Andrew Linzey opens *Animal Theology* with a walk through historical theological comparisons—Barth, Aquinas, Schweitzer, Primatt, Griffiths, Bonhoeffer—indicating the place of animals in some of the major theological expositions in Christian history. Without restating his analyses, he characterizes Schweitzer's reverence of life as comprehensive, universal, and limitless; then he contrasts Barth's position based on Barth's own critique of Schweitzer. Linzey proceeds, then, to question Barth, noting that "what is difficult in Barth is not just that he proposes a fundamental theological distinction between humans and animals, but rather what he wants to deduce from such a distinction. What is so problematic is the way in which God's 'yes' to humankind in the incarnation becomes a 'no' to creation as a whole."[38] Again, the incarnation, for Barth, puts a impenetrable barrier between humans and the rest of the creation. He follows with a similar comparison between Aquinas and Primatt, then between himself and Griffiths. It is in this section that Linzey weaves "rights language" through much of the discussion, particularly the concept of Theos-Rights: "Animals can be wronged because their Creator can be wronged in his creation." In other words, while rights language runs into many hurdles in the animal discussion, Theos-Rights "serves to convey to us that the claims of animals are God-Based claims of justice."[39]

He continues by positing that animals should not only be given moral consideration but also should be given greater consideration; because they are "weak," they should have "moral priority."[40] Linzey calls this the "generosity" paradigm, and in some ways it sounds strikingly familiar to ideas set forth by Scully and Webb: Humans must respond to animals with compassion and dominion; they are our pets and we must consider them in their weakness and from our strength. Indeed, Linzey himself says that one objection to his generosity paradigm is that it "invites a return to the old notions of paternalism and philanthropy, whereas the modern movement for animal liberation is precisely concerned to cast off this framework of nobless oblige."[41] But Linzey doesn't cast out rights language; rather, he suggests that generosity meets some needs and rights meet others.

In a potentially controversial move, Linzey proposes a "liberation theology for animals." As a way of entering into the ideas of "liberation theology" he gives a background, citing Gustavo Gutierrez and Leonardo Boff, two of the most prominent liberation theologians of the late twentieth century. He comes to the conclusion that both Boff and Gutierrez, in the final analysis, present a "constricted and exclusive theology" because its "concept of liberation is too narrow." Even "when confronted . . . with evidence in the form of St. Francis of Assisi and his extension of the moral community to include animals . . . the result is still humanocentrism."

Based on this critique of liberation theologies thus far conceived, Linzey intends to "show that there is a theological basis for animal liberation, indeed that liberation theology itself, properly interpreted, provides it."[42] For Linzey, the issue is a deficient christology, and he proposes a new formulation that extends to the entire creation. From this, he still ends up with humans in a central position, commissioned "to liberate God's creation."[43] But whereas most theological systems, liberation theologies included, focus on a humano-centricity that views humankind as the "only criterion of moral good," he espouses "suffering servant humanism."[44]

In a collaborative effort with Dan Cohn-Sherbok, Linzey suggests that animals not only fit within liberation theology but also "can liberate Jewish and Christian theology."[45] They contend that there are four ways in which con-temporary theology "needs" animals: resisting idolatry, rejecting humanism, repenting of hubris, and identifying innocent suffering. Jewish and Christian theologies suffer from the "attempt to deify the human species by regarding the interests of human beings as the sole, main, or even exclusive concern of God the Creator."[46] Christian theology, in particular, is susceptible to this idolatry because of humanocentric incarnation theologies. Closely related to this is the need to reject humanism because of the inherent limits it places on God as Creator. If the "chief purpose of creation is the making of *Homo sapiens,*" then ideas such as this one, articulated by Karl Barth, become in-grained: "There are no useless insects, but only those whose utility is not yet known to us and has still to be discovered."[47] Rather, the "existence of other communities of life with their own apparent integrity and consciousness of the world should inspire in us not defensive theological utilitarianism, but a search for a doctrine of God the Creator whose creative love has no apparent biological favourites."[48]

"Repenting of hubris" is rather straightforward. Christian theology needs animals to liberate itself "from the perpetual desire of human beings to think more highly of themselves than they should." Here Linzey and Cohn-Sher-bock offer a critique to any ideas of dominion in animal theologies. They state that the "doctrine of 'dominion' has become translated into notions of always 'knowing better' and always 'having the right.' . . . [I]t strikes us as ironical that the one species which has been so unable to exercise any responsible control over its own population should now presume to dictate to all others."[49] Finally, animals can liberate theology by "expanding our understanding of the justice of God"; this is the concept of innocent suffering posited by Linzey and Cohn-Sherbock. A theology that takes animal suffering and pain seriously is one that recognizes Elie Wiesel's oft-quoted and radically important question posed at Auschwitz: "Where is God? Where is He?" In their analysis of Jewish and Christian theologies, they contend that "morally innocent" animals offer a window into God as "pre-eminently present in the suffering of the vulnerable, the undefended, the unprotected, and the innocent."[50]

The concept of innocent suffering segues into Jay McDaniel's *Of God and Pelicans: A Theology of Reverence for Life*. Both McDaniel and McFague take modern scientific understandings of life into consideration, as do most ecological theologies. Ideas of evolution, interconnectedness, and the commonality of the physical materials of life merge to bring about a new cosmology, one that is shared between many religious ecological thinkers and modern scientists. This new cosmology undergirds the thinking of both scholars. And for McDaniel, a God involved in the suffering and death of all beings marks a theology with animals in mind.

In his book McDaniel proposes a process theology formed with relational panentheism in mind that culminates in a biocentric Christianity (as opposed to an anthropocentric one). Relational panentheism, as he describes it, is to believe that "(1) the 'stuff' of which the world consists is not identical to the 'stuff' of which God consists, and (2) that the history of the universe, in generality and detail, is not always expressive of the will or purposes of God, though it may be." The world is "other than God even as it is in God."[51] An experiential example provides a prelude to the conclusion McDaniel draws. As suggested by the title of his book, he tells about the apparent tragedy of the evolutionary requirement for pelicans, as a species, to survive. Female pelicans usually lay two eggs, even though they cannot raise two young. The first chick that hatches attacks the younger, weaker chick, also taking all the food and eventually driving the weaker chick out of the nest. Nine times out of ten, the younger chick "thrashes about in search of food and then dies of abuse or starvation."[52] This entire process leads McDaniel to ask, "But how large is a God for whom some individual organisms are too small?"[53]

In response to this question, and in light of relational panentheism, McDaniel proposes that a "God who suffers only with humans is too small. Our task is to recognize that there are countless crosses in our world, nonhuman as well as human, to which countless victims are involuntarily nailed, often by powers that have nothing to do with human agency."[54] And sometimes these crosses have nothing to do with divine agency, either, a central point in his theology. God is all-loving but not all-powerful. So he, along with process theologians in general, suggest that "the relation between God and the universe is—and has been from a beginningless past—an ongoing inter-action between manifold creative agents: an all-caring, all influential, and all faithful agent, whom we name God, and countless other agents, including ourselves, who collectively form God's body."[55]

As does Linzey, McDaniel brings in the idea of the cosmic Christ present in human and in nonhuman life. For him, the cosmic Christ is the Spirit that lures human and nonhuman organisms "to live from moment to moment with some degree of satisfaction relative to their situations." So even the second pelican chick seeks this satisfaction, and in the "struggle between the two chicks, God is on the side of each, desirous of the well-being of both."[56]

This brings the discussion back to evolution. Process theologians view the emergence of life on Earth as a "fall upward" (thus back to the plight of the second pelican). With the appearance of animal life, suffering as we know it also appeared. McDaniel lays this out clearly:

> Here two questions emerge. Did the benefits of this fall upward outweight [sic] the costs? And was the fall upward willed by God? Process theologians answer yes to both questions. They see the lure of God at work in the evolu-tion of life on Earth, including animal life, and they believe that the benefits of increased creativity and sentience for animals were worth the costs to the rest of creation, to animals themselves, and to God. . . . The costs to God—at least a God who is all-loving—must have been great. In the first place, the beckoning of the world into animal life involved risk, a relinquishment of divine control. . . . In the second place, the luring of the world into animal life involved an increase in divine suffering. If one considers the countless billions of painful experiences suffered by creatures since animal life began, and imagine in each instance that suffering was shared by an all-empathic God, the suffering of God staggers the imagination.

With the "increased capacities for sentience" came, necessarily, "increased capacities for pain."[57] In a similar way Ursula Goodenough, a biologist and author of *Sacred Depths of Nature*, addresses the connections between death and complexity. Simple organisms could simply reproduce, nothing else. In order to have cells that focus on something besides reproduction, such as the cells in the human brain, they must die.[58] So to live as complex animals live, we must also suffer and die. At what cost life?

McDaniel answers this cost with his interpretation of redemption, a redemption that is inclusive of all life and not exclusive in any way to humans. He returns to the pelican again, quoting Rolston: The "luckless backup chick suffers and dies, a minor pelican tragedy, but this sort of thing, amplified over and over, makes nature seem cruel and ungodly."[59] He argues that "even if there is not a renewal after death, the backup chick's life is nevertheless worthwhile, even on his own terms." So we should take care in judging the worthiness of another's life, particularly as nonhumans cannot speak to us, at least not in ways we understand. Second, McDaniel believes that "the ultimate meaning of life lies not in fulfillment of our individual needs . . . but rather in our contribution to the divine life."[60]

Without detailing the rest of this theological system, for which the first section is foundational, I draw from it just a few main points. The "life-centered God" (outlined above) leads to a "life-centered ethic" and a "life-centered spirituality" that lead to a "post-patriarchal Christianity."[61] His thinking culminates in connections with feminist theologies claiming that "lest biocentric Christianity neglect people in its extension of liberation to the nonhuman world, it must drink deeply from the wells of feminist thought."[62] Of course, this is central to my entire thesis because feminisms seek to rethink and reactivate culture away from patriarchal dualisms, including the human/animal binary. Briefly, McDaniel defines a "process postpatriarchal Christianity" as one that recognizes "human beings are by no means the sole locus of value or the sole end of cosmic and terrestrial evolutionary developments. All living beings, not just human beings, have intrinsic value."[63]

In McDaniels' theology, theocentricism, as proposed by Linzey, becomes a biocentric theology. The pelican's role in the creation plays a central role in the theological ideas expressed. So animals are not valued only as subjects in the system, though a system now focused on God instead of humans; they are taken into account fully as a way of trying to comprehend the workings of God, indeed, the very nature of God. And all animals are a part of the very nature of God in both their suffering and in their redemption.

Although not explicitly a theological piece about animals, Sallie McFague's book *The Body of God: An Ecological Theology* provides a complimentary framework for both Linzey and McDaniel. McFague begins by emphasizing that "Christianity is the religion of the incarnation *par excellence.*" But the merging of various complex historical patterns led to a "full-blown distrust of the body."[64] She suggests a return to the incarnational focus of Christianity, specifically to the model of the Body, and the Body of God, for an ecological theology. What would this mean for animals?

First of all, the idea of the creation as the visible body of the invisible deity is not unknown in Western history. But "for the early Christians Christ became the head of the universe and the universe his body, or, more typically, the church became the body with Christ as the head"; thus the model "was narrowed to human beings."[65] The idea of the church as the body of Christ continued to exclude all except for those humans who were Christian. So in the "Christian version of the organic model, the divine . . . is not present in the whole of creation or even in the whole of the human being, but is located in and limited to the rational/spiritual part of the human being, the head."[66]

McFague poses a question to this model: "[W]hat if the organic model did *not* assume a human (male or female) body for its base, but *bodies,* all the diverse, strange, multitude of bodies (matter in all its millions, perhaps billions of forms) that make up the universe?" She asks this with a contemporary scientific understanding of the universe in place since the "fifteen-billion-year evolutionary story does not privilege any particular body, let alone a lately arrived one on a minor planet in an ordinary galaxy (the human body!)." Suddenly, dominion, compassion, and humans as the protectors of all things good and judgers of all things evil goes out the window. Humans are no longer at the center of anything, certainly not at the center of the divine process of creation. Her description of this Body of God is worth quoting at length:

> [O]ur focus would change from ourselves as the center of things to appreciating the awesome, splendid, magnificent diversity of bodies; and, were we then to speak of the universe as God's body, it would not be this or that body, and certainly not a human body, but *all* the bodies that have ever been or ever will be, from quarks and exploding stars to microorganisms and centipedes, rocks, mountains, and water, but not forgetting tortoises, pine trees, buttercups, giraffes, and, of course, human beings in their various shapes, conditions, and colors.[67]

Obviously, animals are as much a part of the body of God as humans.

With this in mind, McFague emphasizes that humans hold a certain place in the scheme of things at this juncture in history. Humans are not more important than any other species; rather, they are radically interrelated and interdependent on all aspects of creation. Although "other than what either the Christian tradition, especially since the Reformation, claims we are or what secular, modern culture allows," both of which contend that humans are the center, humans still carry a particular responsibility. Because of "the wedding of science and technology, we are in a critically important position. We have the knowledge and the power to destroy ourselves as well as many other species." But along with this we "have the knowledge and the power to help the process of the ongoing creation continue."[68] In other words, humans do not have dominion over and do not hold an elevated place in the hierarchy of the cosmos; indeed, such a hierarchy is in and of itself a faulty perception. But humans do have a responsibility because of the technologies and ideologies that shape our culture.

In terms of animals, this means that humans need to think "beyond democracy to biocracy, seeing ourselves as one species among millions of other species on a planet that is our common home." Such thinking should not be sentimental, she contends, and does not "emerge merely from a fondness for charming panda bears or baby seals." We must be "decentered and recentered . . . no longer the whole point of the show, as Western culture and Christian tradition have often implied, but we have emerged as bearing heavy responsibilities for the well-being of the whole." Refusing to accept this place is nothing less than sinful.[69]

Now, this is a metaphor in her estimation; the world is not actually God's body, but metaphorically so. Then again, all religious language is metaphor. While some philosophers and theologians employ language to make humans the only ones close to the divine, others employ language to remind us that we are part of a larger cosmic whole. That is the purpose of McFague's image: The "body of God is not *a* body, but all the different, peculiar, particular bodies around us."[70]

Conclusions

> Therefore, let those who bring about wonderful things
> In their big, dark books
> Take an animal to help them.
> The life within the animal
> Will give them strength in turn.
> For equality gives strength,
> In all things and at all times.
> —Meister Eckhart[71]

In a powerful essay, "The Universe Responds," Alice Walker writes about noticing animals in her midst. If she admires the squirrel in the branches outside her window, soon there are three or four squirrels. If she looks into the eyes of a raccoon at night, it looks back, and soon there is a family of raccoons living in the tree. And then "there are the deer, who know they need never, ever fear me."[72]

And thus it seems to be when looking through the hidden stacks for the other histories of Christianity. When one begins to look for animals, they appear in droves (or herds, or flocks, or packs). Accompanying saints, begging from the eucharistic table, healing the sick, and waiting for a blessing. But they are not there simply at the request of humans, as several contemporary theologians remind us. Animals live at the center of the incarnation of God and, indeed, are part of the body of God, as fully as are human beings. By opening our eyes to see them in rituals and theologies, as well as in everyday ethical concerns, Christianity might find one of its many holes filled.

Epilogue

Any complete feminist piece, and surely any ecofeminist piece, is strength-
ened, in my opinion, by a brief statement submitted by the author about who
she is, where her roots are planted, and why she chose to care about what she
wrote. In other words, I close this environmental history/historical theology
bricolage with the subjective, with my position.

I grew up in the arms of Christianity, specifically, mainline Protestant
U.S. Christianity in the late twentieth century. Certainly my formation in
this tradition was progressive. My father was the only minister I knew, and
he worked (and still works) tirelessly on antiracism and peace initiatives in
the church and the world. Still, it was and is a patriarchal Christianity in
many ways that were not always transparent. And in addition to my sister
and brother, our household always included beloved animals—a cat, dogs,
birds, hamsters, and fish. The occasional rat family or crawdad community
came home with me from school, and my mother deserves much credit for
helping me take care of these critters. The deaths of these animals were taken
seriously, and a small animal cemetery occupied the top of the hill in our
side yard. There are still animals in all of these family households—among
the most loved animal companions in the world, I'm sure.

But there is something else, another aspect of this combination, that must
have influenced the development of the ideas in this book. Was it singing
"The Lord said to Noah, there's gonna be a floody floody / get those animals
out of the muddy, muddy" during Vacation Bible School as a child? Was it
camping under the stars at Assateague Island, surrounded by the beauty of
those wild horses, on church youth group retreats? Was it noticing that the
small sheep at the bottom of the stained glass window in the church where I

spent so very many hours were so far down that you couldn't see them from the sanctuary? Was it staring into the eyes of the small cow that the caretakers of the church campground were going to slaughter? Or was it singing "Joyful, Joyful We Adore Thee" with all of its fabulous nature imagery—field and forest, vale and mountain, flowery meadow, flashing sea, chanting bird, and flowing fountain? It may well have been watching *Brother Sun and Sister Moon,* a movie about the life of Saint Francis, in the church's fellowship hall when I was a young teenager.

Certainly, throughout my life and in my memory, animals were not "other" or outside of Christianity. Although they weren't in the center of it, neither were they excluded. And animals were, often, in the center of my life. So from these positions I dove into the study of the history of the Christian tradition and looked for animals; everybody else was doing a fine job looking for humans there (though certainly some humans get much more attention than others). The amazing thing was, I found animals much more easily than one might imagine. It just took a bit of reading between the lines, looking with eyes focused on a different subject, and, I believe, asking the animals to find me as well.

As I completed the first draft of this manuscript, a story hit the news about a dog in Kenya. This dog, a stray bitch with a litter of her own, apparently saved an abandoned baby. According to a human witness, "I saw a dog carrying a baby wrapped in a black dirty cloth as it crossed the road." The dog then placed the baby in a "wooden and corrugated-iron shack," where residents found the infant "lying next to the dog and her own pup" (*New York Times,* May 12, 2005). She was then named Mkombozi (Savior) for saving the human child. This followed a story several years earlier of a female gorilla protecting a human child who had fallen into her enclosure at a zoo in the United States.

There is too much tragic cultural baggage in the story of Mkombozi to unpack at this juncture. But it turns me back to stories of animals and saints with ravens feeding hermits and lions living side by side with ascetics. Certainly these might be embellishments, their purpose focused on the morality of humans who hear the legends. Still, if a dog takes a human baby to care for with her pups in the early twenty-first century, might not a greyhound save an infant from a snake and then be considered a saint in his own right? If a dog takes a human baby into her den, might not a lioness let Jesus into her den? Just an image—and a reality.

Notes

Preface

1. Bataille 22.
2. Bataille, chapter 3 on sacrifice.
3. Waldau and Patton 2.
4. Bekoff 76. Bekoff's work served as the focus for a joint session of "Animals and Religion" and "Religion and Science" at the AAR meeting in 2004. Papers from the session appear in the spring 2006 issue of *Zygon*.

Chapter 1: Weaving and Roaring

1. Berger, *About Looking* 2.
2. An alternate spelling is Zopitus. The research for this portion of the text was conducted by the author in May–June 2002 in Loreto Aprutino, Italy.
3. Recently a newspaper article reported that a letter dated October 12, 1710, confirmed the identity of the relics, thus reestablishing the significance of the ritual. See Orlando D'Angelo, "San Zopito non e piu leggenda," *Messaggero*, Dec. 27, 2000. This continued validation of the "legend" speaks to the significance of the ritual even to this day.
4. These descriptions are taken from discussions with ritual participants and from various descriptions of the event. For a brief description with images, see the Abruzzo 2000 website: www.abruzzo2000.com.
5. Humans are animals, of course. In literature dealing with the cultural construction and reality of "other-than-human" animals, terms to use are debated. For ease of writing, "animals" throughout this work refer to other-than-human animals, but the author constantly keeps in mind that humans are also fully and completely animals.
6. Linzey, introduction to Linzey and Yamamoto.
7. Singer 3.

8. The phrase in quotations refers to the above-cited essay, "Why Look at Animals?" in Berger, *About Looking.*

9. I refer to Christianity as the largest recognized religious system because, arguably, global capitalism is the largest religious system, in the guise of an economic system, that has or probably will ever circle the earth.

10. Derrida, "Animal that Therefore I Am" 400.

11. Miles 8.

12. Ibid. 11.

13. Ibid. 188–90.

14. Miles, Appendix lays out this entire position in concise terms.

15. Schmitt 8.

16. Adams, *Neither Man nor Beast,* 198.

17. Hobgood-Oster, "Ecofeminism," *The Encyclopedia of Religion and Nature* (New York: Continuum, 2005).

18. Mulvey 11.

19. DeLauretis 3.

20. Derrida, "Sending," 306.

21. Ibid.

22. Foucault xxiii.

23. Ibid. 14.

24. Cited in Adams, *Neither Man nor Beast* 178; translation from the Greek by Philip Hopkins.

25. Baker 211.

26. See Carol Adams's work on the absent referent in Adams, *Sexual Politics of Meat.*

27. Carol Adams, in her book *The Sexual Politics of Meat,* analyzes representations of animals in the "meat" industry and of the connections between these representations and the female body.

28. For an interesting analysis of this issue, see Scully.

29. Berger, *About Looking,* 5.

30. Ibid. 6–7.

31. Adams, *Sexual Politics of Meat* 42.

32. Bauckham 4.

33. This quotation is from Augustine's *De Genesi ad litteram imperfectus liber* (16.55). For a recent analysis of Augustine and animals, see Waldau 191–201.

34. Schmitt 7.

35. Schweitzer 118, quoted in Linzey and Regan.

Chapter 2: Guardians of the Gateway

1. Germond and Livet 149.

2. Various scholars study this most recent syncretism of culture and Christianity: David R. Loy, "The Religion of the Market," *Journal of the American Academy of Religion* 65 (2): 275–90; Michael Budde and Robert Brimlow, *Christianity Incorporated* (Grand Rapids: Brazos, 2002); R. Laurence Moore, *Selling God* (New York: Oxford UP, 1994).

3. At the beginning of the twenty-first century, Christianities are the primary religious

system for approximately one-third of the human population—two billion of the earth's six billion people. Biocentric Christianities, therefore, are requisite to shift religious sensibilities in the midst of the impending, and already present, environmental crisis. Numerous theologians are contributing to this transformation: Sallie McFague, Jay McDaniel, John Cobb, Andrew Linzey, Rosemary Radford Ruether, Karen Baker-Fletcher, Larry Rasmussen, and many others.

4. Visitors can see the remains of the Gaia temple in the foundation of San Ruffino because of extensive archaeological work completed in the last few decades.

5. Germond and Livet 122.

6. See the following works by Marija Gimbutas: *Language of the Goddess, Civilization of the Goddess,* and *The Living Goddess* (Berkeley: U of California P, 1999).

7. Gimbutas, *Language of the Goddess* 107–8.

8. For information on the Lion Gate of Mycenae, see George E. Mylonas, *Mycenae: Rich in Gold* (Athens: Edkotike Athenon SA, 1983); also see John Gray, *Near Eastern Mythology* (New York: Peter Bedrick, 1985).

9. Callou, Samzun, and Zivie 212.

10. Schimmel 34–35.

11. Lawler 89.

12. While editing the final version of this text, *The Lion, the Witch, and the Wardrobe,* the book in the *Chronicles of Narnia* that introduces Aslan, came out as a feature film. So again, and in a different form, animals enter the popular Christian imagination for another generation of story hearers.

13. Adolf 51.

14. Thomas Mathews, *The Clash of the Gods* (Princeton: Princeton UP, 1993) 45.

15. *The Ante-Nicene Fathers* (New York: Charles Scribner's Sons, 1926) (hereafter cited as *ANF*), vii, 158.

16. The term "pagan" is problematized and defined below.

17. *ANF,* vi, 420.

18. *ANF,* vi. 468.

19. Kyle 43.

20. Ibid. 103.

21. Ibid. 77.

22. Wiedeman 60.

23. Ibid. 16.

24. Hughes 106.

25. Germond and Livet 122.

26. The literature here is too large to note, but a place to begin looking for information on the links between ancient pagan and neopagan movements in Europe is Jones and Pennick.

27. See the works by Meeks and Stegeman.

28. For definitions of "paganism," see Jones and Pennick; MacMullen and Lane vii–ix.

29. Chidester 166.

30. Beda, chap. xxxii, 58.

31. See Chidester 167, from Bede.

32. Gregory 239.

33. See also Berger, *Goddess Obscured,* and Milis.
34. Szoverffy 111–22.
35. Green 193–94.
36. See Jones and Pennick.
37. See Milis 6–7. "Our own inclination is to regard the Middle Ages as a time during which, over a long period and mainly passively, paganism resisted the introduction of the new faith, which had the backing of an ever-expanding church."
38. Van Engen 549–50.
39. Mathews, *Clash of the Gods,* 48.
40. Aquinas 1.47.1
41. Ibid. 1.64.1.
42. Ibid. 1.65.3
43. Marsilio Ficino, *Platonic Theology,* quoted in Glacken 463.
44. Merchant xvi.
45. Oelschlaeger 76–77.
46. Horkheimer and Adorno, *Dialectic of Enlightenment,* quoted in King 460.
47. William Harvey published *An Anatomical Study of the Motion fo the Heart and Blood in Animals* in 1628, establishing the idea that the heart pumps blood throughout the body and then recirculates it.
48. Descartes 317.
49. Merchant designates this as Bacon's "nonegalitarian philosophy" (177).
50. Bacon 159.
51. Descartes 140–41.
52. Linzey and Clarke 17. From Thomas Hobbes, "De Homine," *Man and Citizen,* trans. Bernard Gert (London: Harverster, 1976).
53. Ickert 92.
54. Ibid. 95.
55. Huff 68.
56. Quoted in Huff 69–70 (Calvin, Institutes, 1.14,20, 1.16.6).
57. Ibid. 73.
58. Ibid. 70.
59. Quoted in Ryder 56.
60. Bentham, quoted in Linzey and Clarke 136.
61. Descartes 1:142–43.
62. Darwin, referenced in Waldau 20.
63. Ibid.
64. Spiegel 15.
65. *Peaceable Kingdom* documentary.
66. Albright 145.
67. Some of these critiques take visual narrative form, such as *Peaceable Kingdom.*
68. Fraser 636.
69. Albright 146.
70. This specific wording comes from H.B. 326, Texas State Legislature, Mar. 2005.
71. Fox, "Agriculture" 557.
72. Adams, *Sexual Politics of Meat* 52.
73. Daly and Cobb, *For the Common Good,* among other works.

Chapter 3: *The Ephesian Lion and Clay Sparrows*

1. "Acts of Paul and Thecla" 351–52.

2. The "Bible" refers, throughout, to the Hebrew scriptures (the Christian Old Testament) and the Christian New Testament. All biblical quotations in this book are taken from the New Revised Standard Version for consistency.

3. Several of the best sources are Linzey and Yamamoto; Pinches and McDaniel; Webb; Charles Birch, William Eakin, and Jay McDaniel, eds., *Liberating Life: Contemporary Approaches to Ecological Theology* (Maryknoll: Orbis, 1990); Carol Adams and Marjorie Procter-Smith, "Taking Life or 'Taking on Life'?" *Ecofeminism and the Sacred* (New York: Continuum, 1995); and Norman C. Habel, ed., *The Earth Bible,* 5 vols. (Sheffield, England: Sheffield Academic, 2000–2002), various essays.

4. The case of *The Da Vinci Code,* by Dan Brown, speaks to this interest when texts are made available to those who are unaware of their existence. This popular novel introduces, albeit in a less than historically critical fashion, apocryphal texts such as the Gospel of Thomas and the Gospel of Mary. As of January 2005, *The Da Vinci Code* was number one on the *New York Times* bestseller list and had been on the list for ninety-three weeks.

5. Ehrman, *After the New Testament* 1.

6. Much of this happened through popular literature such as *The Da Vinci Code,* but the widespread cultural impact was amazing. I was invited to numerous churches and secular groups (mostly women's groups) to do presentations on the historical Mary Magdalene after the popular remembering of her began in the late twentieth century.

7. Alter 14.

8. For an interesting analysis of Genesis 9, see Olley 9.

9. Bauckham 4.

10. Ibid. 8.

11. Ibid. 14.

12. Ibid. 20.

13. Ibid. 21.

14. Linzey, *Animal Gospel* 13–14. At this point Linzey is referring to a sermon preached by Cardinal Newman in 1842.

15. "Infancy Gospel of Thomas" 83.

16. Ibid. 76.

17. Ibid. 81.

18. Ibid. 94.

19. Ibid. 95.

20. Ibid.

21. Ibid. 97–98.

22. Dunkerley 143–44.

23. Dunkerley points out that a German writer, Julius Boehmer, "in a collection of Early Christian parallels to the New Testament" includes this account, which he drew "from an earlier writer, but failed to trace its history owing to the latter's death." Supposedly it exists in a Coptic Bible manuscript in the Paris Library, but searches there proved unsuccessful (143).

24. Fiorenza 53.

25. The first list of the twenty-seven books contained in the final, official canon appeared in 367 CE in a letter sent by Athanasius to his churches.

26. Eusebius includes an appendix with the "Canon of the New Testament" in his *The History of the Church from Christ to Constantine* (New York: Penguin, 1984), 424.

27. Thompson 31–32.

28. "Acts of Paul and Thecla" 277.

29. The Acts of Paul exists only in large fragments. A widely accepted compilation is available in *The Apocryphal New Testament,* ed. J. K. Elliott (Oxford: Oxford UP, 1993).

30. Acts of Paul in C. Schmidt, *Praxeis Paulou* (Hamburg: Augustin, 1936), 38–43, p. 5 of the Hamburg papyrus; first English translation, Metzger 11–21. Also cited in Grant.

31. Elliott 378–79.

32. Acts of Thecla, chaps. 28, 33.

33. "The Passion of the Holy Martyrs Perpetua and Feliticas," from *ANF.*

34. "Letter of Ignatius to the Romans," *ANF* 73–77.

35. Grant 17.

36. "Passio sanctorum apostolorum Petri et Pauli," *ANF* 8:481.

37. Elliott 350.

38. Metzger 17.

39. Ferreiro 45.

40. Ehrman, *Lost Christianities* 203.

41. Barnstone and Meyer 274.

42. Jonas 32.

43. Williams 26.

44. Robinson 173.

45. Barnstone and Meyer 269.

46. Ibid. 274.

47. Ibid. 269–70.

48. Robinson 126.

49. Ibid. 128.

50. Ibid. 135.

51. Ibid. 183–84.

52. That stated, there are glimpses of hope for females in these texts. Some forms of early Christian gnosticism provide an odd example of a religious system that is empowering for women but not for other species. Usually these dualisms are wiped out together.

53. Origen, *Contra Celsum* 4:531.

54. Ibid. 4:532.

55. Arnobius, "Against the Heathen," *ANF* 6:520–21.

56. Lactantius, "On the Workmanship of God," *ANF* 7:282.

Chapter 4: Counted among the Saints

1. Jacobus de Voragine, *The Golden Legend Readings on the Saints,* Princeton UP, 1993. vol. 1, 84–85.

2. Voragine 84–85.

3. Bitel 213.

4. McBrien 6.

5. Kieckhefer 6.

6. McBrien 6–8.

7. One reason for the sheer numbers of saints canonized is that John Paul II included several large groups of martyrs. See the Vatican News for specific lists of saints, http://www.vatican.va/news_services/liturgy/saints/index_saints_en.html (accessed September 10, 2004).

8. Davies 173–74. From *The Voyage of Brendan.*

9. Davies 180.

10. Donatello, *Miracle of the Mule,* bronze, parcel gilt, Basilica del Santo, Padua.

11. These images have been gathered during research sessions in Italy. See image 4, referenced in chapter 2, for the Siena baptistery portrayal.

12. *Little Flowers of St. Francis* 37.

13. Armstrong 59.

14. *Little Flowers of St. Francis* 37.

15. Voragine 2:266–67.

16. Ibid. 2:127–28.

17. *Flammarion Iconographic Guides* 154.

18. Doran 93.

19. The Cathedral of Siena is adorned with thirteenth-century sculptures of Nicola Pisano. Animals are portrayed throughout his series of sculptures depicting scenes from the life of Jesus.

20. See the entire chapter, titled "The Granted Image"

21. Trout 286.

22. Ibid. 287

23. This fabulous basilica is located south of Ravenna on the eastern coast of Italy.

24. See chapter 2, this volume.

25. Voragine 229.

26. From the *Life of Macarius of Alexandria,* quoted in Vivian 487.

27. Ibid. 91.

28. Ibid. 2:148–49

29. Ibid. 151.

30. Ibid. 187.

31. From Macarius's *Virtues,* quoted in Vivian 486–87.

32. Montalembert, 2:212.

33. Ibid. 2:227.

34. Kienzle n.p.

35. For a history of bestiaries, see Clark and McMunn and McCulloch. I deal with this genre only briefly here because it has been addressed in detail elsewhere.

36. Yamamoto 82.

37. Yamamoto 81–82.

38. Kienzle n.p.

39. McCulloch 70.

40. Clark and McMunn 4.

41. Di Monte Santa Maria 47–50.

42. Kienzle n.p.

43. Hildegard of Bingen 495.

44. Linzey, *Animal Theology* 66–67.

45. Ruether and Keller 3.

Chapter 5: The Granted Image

1. *Michael,* dir. Nora Ephron, dist. New Line, 1996.

2. For more information, see Coppinger and Coppinger; Thurston; and Vila and Savolainen. Vila and Savolainen proposed the time span of one hundred thousand years based on DNA research; this theory proved controversial.

3. Stanley Coren emphasizes this point: "How many times has the fate of a man, or even a nation, hung from the collar of a dog? Had it not been for dogs, the last imperial house of China might not have fallen; Columbus's first attempts at colonizing the Americas not have been so successful; some of Wagner's operas might never have been written; the American Revolution might not have been fought; the freeing of the American slaves might have been delayed for decades; the way that we educate deaf children might be different; and great and well-loved books like *Ivanhoe* might never have been written" (1).

4. Thurston 5–7

5. Haraway 29.

6. See Coppinger and Coppinger, "Part I: The Evolution of the Basic Dog," for a critique of artificial selection theories.

7. Dogs such as the dingo (Australia and sub-Saharan Africa), Canaan dog (Middle East), North Carolina wild dog and Navajo dog (North America), and others, mostly just "mutts," fill this category of village dog.

8. For a broad outline of the work in the field of archaeozoology, see Crockford.

9. See Allman.

10. Coppinger and Coppinger 21.

11. Crockford vii.

12. Haraway 32.

13. Companion species can refer to everything from agricultural species (such as corn) to animal species that are often used for food (such as cattle or sheep depending on culture) to animals that work (such as oxen and dogs).

14. Haraway 5.

15. Brewer, Clark, and Phillips 43.

16. Herodotus, *Histories* 2:65–67.

17. Miziolek 68.

18. Clark 116.

19. Nigosian.

20. Stager 30; correction in *Biblical Archaeology Review* 17 (6): 18.

21. Wapnish and Hesse 58.

22. Zooarchaeologists Wapnish and Hesse confirm that the dogs died of natural causes and the mortality profile is similar to that of urban dog populations; in other words, the high percentage of puppies and subadult dogs is anticipated with natural causes. Stager 31–32.

23. Ibid. 38.

24. Wapnish and Hesse 69.

25. Livingstone 58.

26. Ibid. 58–59.

27. Originally Cerberus was depicted as having fifty or one hundred heads, but the most common depictions morph into a three-headed dog.

28. Smith 82. These festivals took place from the ninth through the sixth centuries BCE.

29. Ibid.

30. Houston 22.

31. Examples are too numerous to quote in full. Other passages include Exodus 22:31, 1 Kings 14:11, Proverbs 26:11, and 2 Samuel 3:8.

32. Goodfriend 383.

33. Ibid. 388.

34. See Van de Sandt 223–46, for a fascinating explanation of the relationships between these two early Christian texts.

35. "Infancy Gospel of Thomas" 103.

36. Hennecke 291–92.

37. Ibid. 294–95.

38. Coren 292.

39. *The Baptism of Jesus* by Pietro de Mera in the Chapel of the Basilica Giacomo Salomoni; Leandro Bassano's *San Giacinto pass moracolosamente un fiume* (1608–10) in the Chapel of our Lady of Peace.

40. This image is also titled *The Church Militant and Triumphant* and was painted c. 1366–68.

41. Meiss 70.

42. Tappert 38.

43. Mancinelli 15.

44. Lewine 86.

45. The image is currently housed in Saint Lawrence at Wormley in Hertfordshire, England (a provincial church); its original setting may have been a convent in a village near Verona (see Joannides and Sachs 695). It remains an image of popular devotion.

46. Ibid. 696.

47. See image 9 in chapter 5 for another example of art in situ in the Basilica Dei Santi Giovanni e Paolo.

48. Rosand 163.

49. Ibid. 164.

50. Worthen 707.

51. The four I have seen in Venice that include dogs are in these locations and were painted on these dates: San Stefano (originally painted for Santa Margherita), c. 1580; San Simeon Grande, c. 1562; Scuola Grande di San Rocco, c. 1579–81; San Giorgio Maggiore, c. 1592–94 (probably one of the final images painted by Tintoretto).

52. Worthen 717–18.

53. Valcanouver and Pignatti 146.

54. Rosand 209.

55. My translation.
56. This painting initially hung in San Marcuola (see Valcanouver and Pignatti 23)
57. Davies 142.
58. Bitel 213.
59. Voragine 2:11.
60. Ameisenowa 43–44.
61. Thurston 65.
62. Jamieson 35.
63. For a detailed examination of comparative templates of this tale, see Schmitt 40–67.
64. Hausman and Hausman 56. Also translated as "I am as sorry and remorseful as the man who slew his greyhound." (Coren 33).
65. William Robert Spencer, "Beth-Gelert," in Coren 27–33.
66. Schmitt 5.
67. Ibid. 18.
68. McBrien 7.
69. Tappert 421.
70. Sluhovsky 1397–98.
71. For a careful analysis of this imagery, see Marrow.
72. Crossan 127.
73. Leach 208.
74. Kolenbrander 5.
75. Haraway 5.

Chapter 6: Animals Return to the Sanctuary

1. Text from the Blessing of the Animals and Shelter, Georgetown, Texas, Apr. 30, 2005 (I officiated at this blessing).
2. Geertz 112.
3. Ibid. 112.
4. Smith 476.
5. Ibid.
6. Smith 479.
7. Ibid. 480.
8. Prayer from "Saint Francis and the Blessing of Animals," *Catholic Culture,* www.catholicculture.org.
9. There are numerous histories of pet keeping, including Harriet Ritvo, "Pride and Pedgree," *Victorian Studies,* Winter 1986, 227–53.
10. The description goes into great detail, so I chose to quote selectively.
11. McMurrouch 83–86.
12. Ibid. 86.
13. The difference here depends on whether one counts the initial founding of the street in 1781 or the rehabilitation and reconstruction of the historic district, dating to 1930. Sources disagree on whether or not the blessing took place before the reconstruction.

14. See Estrada 15. See www.olvera-street.com/blessing_of_the_animals.html (accessed October 10, 2004).

16. Linzey, *Animal Gospel* 63.

17. Ibid. 66. From Evelyn Underhill, "Letter to C. S. Lewis," in Williams, *Letters of Evelyn Underhill.*

18. Research for this section of the paper took place at the cathedral in October 2004.

19. All quotations from the liturgy are taken directly from the bulletin distributed at the cathedral.

20. This spatial relationship was announced by the dean of the cathedral at the beginning of the service.

21. These number estimates were suggested by the head deacon.

22. Lorena Mongelli, "Blessed are the Beasts at St. John," *New York Post,* Oct. 7, 2002.

23. Susan Cannon, email interview with author, July 14, 2004.

24. "AC&C Newsletter" (Animal Care and Control of New York City), Sept. 2004. It should be noted that this is a significant decrease and AC&C is working toward making New York a "no-kill" city.

25. The official designation of this church is the Cathedral Church of Saint Peter and Saint Paul in the City and Episcopal Diocese of Washington.

26. Assistant Verger G. Stanley Utterback, personal interview with author, Oct. 4, 2004.

27. These figures come from Internet research and personal contact with congregations. The most comprehensive list in one place can be found at http://www.americancatholic .org.

28. For example, in the Austin, Texas, area I have found only one official listing on the American Catholic site but have attended at least ten different blessings of animals personally.

29. Text provided by Central Christian Church, Dallas, Texas.

30. "Some people brought ashes of deceased pets" (Jack Grubbs, Potomac Falls Episcopal Church, Potomac Falls, Virginia).

31. For ease of reference I chose not to footnote each response. However, I do have a copy of this chapter with each response noted and can provide that for any interested researchers. These are the congregations from whom responses were included in the text: Potomac Falls Episcopal Church (Potomac Falls, Va.), Shadow Hills Presbyterian Church (Sunland, Calif.), King of Peace Episcopal Church (Kingsland, Ga.), Unity Church of Practical Christianity (Grand Rapids, Mich.), Holy Spirit Church (Fremont, Calif.), Saint Peter's Episcopal Church (Chicago), Historic Trinity Lutheran Church (Detroit), Christ the King Church (Mesa, Ariz.), Central Christian Church (Disciples of Christ) (Dallas, Tex.), San Ramon Valley United Methodist Church (Alamo, Calif.), St. Paul's Anglican Church (Manuka, Australia, the only congregation outside of the United Church), Shepherd of the Desert Lutheran Church (Barstow, Calif.), St. Timothy's Episcopal Church (Perrysburg, Ohio), First United Methodist Church (Hastings, Neb.), St. Martin's in the Pines (Birmingham, Ala.), and St. Peter's Episcopal Church (Chicago).

32. St. Timothy's Episcopal Church, Perrysburg, Ohio.

33. For more information, see http://www.kingofpeace.org.

34. For more information, see http://www.hautedogs.org.

35. *Manila Times,* Sunday, Oct. 12, 2003.

36. See http://www.holycrosscatholicchurch.org/School/Blessing_of%20the_Pets/Blessing_of_the_pets.htm (accessed October 15, 2004).

37. Bell 35.

38. Berger, *About Looking* 21.

39. Ibid. 24.

40. Cunningham 34.

41. Frye 67.

42. Marvin 5.

43. Frye 74.

44. Campora 85.

45. Wintz 49.

46. Very Reverend Dr. James A. Kowalski, dean, Cathedral of St. John the Divine, electronic interview with author, June 22, 2004.

47. Kountze, *Kiplinger's Personal Finance,* July 2004, 58 (7): 38.

48. See the APPMA for statistical data. This source is also used by the Humane Society of the United States for their data presentation. See http://www.appma.org/press_industrytrends.asp (accessed September 15, 2004).

49. In 1994, the pet industry accounted for $17 billion and grew to a projected $34.3 billion in 2004, according to the American Pet Products Manufacturers Association and reported in *USA Today Magazine* 133.2715 (Dec. 2004): 7.

50. "Death Toll Continues to Rise," World Farm Animals Day 2004 press release, Sept. 25, 2004.

Chapter 7: Animals Are Good to Think

1. Linzey, *Animal Gospel* 75.

2. This is requoted in Linzey's introduction to *Animals on the Agenda* xv.

3. Aquinas, Question 64

4. Calvin, quoted in Linzey and Regan 21.

5. Linzey and Yamamoto xv.

6. This phrase was on a poster in a classroom in which feminist studies courses were taught at Vanderbilt when I was in graduate school there. The first course I took from Sallie McFague happened to be in that room.

7. Descartes 1:141.

8. Pelikan 63. For an interesting analysis of this idea see Pelikan 48–70.

9. Calvin 91.

10. Santmire 122.

11. Webb 177.

12. Ibid. 109.

13. Ibid. 3.

14. Ibid. 98.

15. Ibid. 100.

16. Ibid. 101.

17. Ibid. 124.

18. Ibid. 168.

19. Ibid. 173.

20. Scully 24.

21. Ibid. 287.

22. Ibid. xii.

23. Ibid. xi–xii

24. Ibid. 71.

25. Ibid.

26. Ibid. 57.

27. Ibid. 91.

28. Ibid. 100.

29. Ibid. 260.

30. Ibid. 9.

31. Ibid. 296.

32. Ibid. 349.

33. Ibid. 398.

34. Webb xi.

35. Mackinnon 265.

36. Ibid. 272.

37. See www.petfinder.com/shelters/gone4thedogsrescue.html, posted as of May 2005; author unknown.

38. Linzey, *Animal Theology* 9.

39. Ibid. 27.

40. Ibid. 28.

41. Ibid. 41.

42. Ibid. 67.

43. Ibid. 71.

44. Ibid. 72.

45. This is the title of chapter 6 in Linzey and Cohn-Sherbok.

46. Ibid. 118.

47. Quoted by Linzey and Cohn-Sherbok 122.

48. Ibid. 123.

49. Ibid. 124.

50. Ibid. 128–29.

51. McDaniel 27.

52. McDaniel points to Holmes Rolston III, who related this story to him (19).

53. Ibid. 21.

54. Ibid. 29.

55. Ibid. 35.

56. Ibid. 39.

57. Ibid. 40–41.

58. Goodenough 148–49.

59. McDaniel 47.

60. Ibid.

61. These are the titles of chapters 2, 3, and 4 of McDaniel's *Of God and Pelicans.*
62. Ibid. 113.
63. Ibid. 139.
64. McFague 14.
65. Ibid. 32.
66. Ibid. 35.
67. Ibid. 37–38.
68. Ibid. 108.
69. Ibid. 110–12.
70. Ibid. 211.
71. From *Meditations with Meister Eckhart,* quoted in ibid. 98.
72. Walker 309.

Bibliography

"Acts of Paul and Thecla." *Apocryphal New Testament* 350–89.

Adams, Carol. *Neither Man nor Beast: Feminism and the Defense of Animals.* New York: Continuum, 1995.

———. *The Sexual Politics of Meat: A Feminist-Vegetarian Critical Theory.* New York: Continuum, 1990.

Adolf, Helen. "The Ass and the Harp." *Speculum* 25.1 (Jan. 1950): 49–57.

Ahl, Diane Cole. *Benozzo Gozzoli.* New Haven: Yale UP, 1996.

Aikema, Bernard. *Jacopo Bassano and His Public: Moralizing Pictures in an Age of Reform, ca. 1535–1600.* Trans. Andrew P. McCormick. Princeton: Princeton UP, 1996.

Albright, Jack. "History and Future of Animal Welfare Science." *Journal of Applied Animal Welfare Science* 1.2 (1988): 145–66.

Allman, John. *Evolving Brains.* New York: Scientific American Library, 2000.

Alter, Robert. "Balaam and the Ass." *Kenyon Review* 24.4 (Fall 2004): 6–32.

Ameisenowa, Zofia. "Animal-Headed Gods, Evangelists, Saints and Righteous Men." *Journal of the Warburg and Courtauld Institutes* 12 (1949): 21–45.

Armstrong, Edward A. *Saint Francis: Nature Mystic; The Derivation and Significance of the Nature Stories in the Franciscan Legend.* Berkeley: U of California P, 1973.

Aquinas, Thomas. *Summa Theologica.* Trans. Fathers of the English Dominican Province. Westminster, Md.: Christian Classics, 1981. Rpt. of New York: Benziger Brothers, 1947–48.

Bacon, Francis. *Essays and New Atlantis.* New York: W. J. Black, 1942.

Baker, Steve. *Picturing the Beast: Animals, Identity, and Representation.* Urbana: U of Illinois P, 2001.

Barnstone, Willis, and Marvin Meyer, eds. *The Gnostic Bible.* Boston: Shambhala, 2003.

Bataille, Georges. *Theory of Religion.* Trans. Robert Hurly. New York: Zone Books, 1989.

Bauckham, Richard. "Jesus and the Wild Animals (Mark 1:13): A Christological Image for an Ecological Age." *Jesus of Nazareth: Lord and Christ (Essays on the Historical*

Jesus and New Testament Christology). Ed. Joel Green and Max Turner. Grand Rapids: Eerdmans, 1994. 3–21.

Beda Venerabilis. *Bede's Ecclesiastical History of England, Also the Anglo-Saxon Chronicle.* Ed. J. A. Giles. London: George Bell & Sons, 1903.

Bekoff, Marc. "Animal Passions and Beastly Virtues." *Zygon* 41.1 (Mar. 2006): 75–108.

Bell, Catherine. *Ritual Theory, Ritual Practice.* New York: Oxford UP, 1992.

Berger, John. *About Looking.* New York: Pantheon Books, 1980.

Berger, Pamela. *The Goddess Obscured: Transformation of the Grain Protectress from Goddess to Saint.* Boston: Beacon, 1985.

Bitel, Lisa. "Body of a Saint, Story of a Goddess: Origins of the Brigidine Tradition." *Textual Practice* 16.2 (2002): 209–28.

Bratton, Susan. "The Original Desert Solitaire: Early Christian Monasticism and Wilderness." *Environmental Ethics* 10.1 (1988): 31–53.

Brewer, Douglas, Terence Clark, and Adrian Phillips. *Dogs in Antiquity: Anubis to Cerberus, the Origins of the Domestic Dog.* Warminster: Aris & Phillips, 2001.

Bynum, Caroline Walker, Stevan Harrell, and Paula Richman, eds. *Gender and Religion: On the Complexity of Symbols.* Boston: Beacon, 1986.

Calvin, John. *Selections from His Writings.* Ed. John Dillenberger. Ann Arbor, Mich: American Academy of Religion, 1975.

Campora, Ralph. "Zoos and Eyes: Contesting Captivity and Seeking Successor Practices." *Society and Animals: Journal of Human-Animal Studies* 13.1 (2005): 69–88.

Callou, Cecile, Anaick Samzun, and Alain Zivie. "A Lion Found in the Egyptian Tomb of Maia." *Nature* 427 (Jan. 2004): 211–12.

Chidester, David. *Christianity: A Global History.* San Francisco: HarperSanFrancisco: 2000.

Clark, Peter. *Zoroastrianism.* Brighton: Sussex Academic, 1998.

Clark, Willene, and Meradith McMunn, eds. *Beasts and Birds of the Middle Ages: The Bestiary and Its Legacy.* Philadelphia: U of Pennsylvania P, 1989.

Cohen, Simona. "Animals in the Paintings of Titian: A Key to Hidden Meanings." *Gazette des Beaux-Arts* 132.1558 (Nov. 1998): 193–212.

Coren, Stanley. *The Pawprints of History: Dogs and the Course of Human Events.* New York: Free Press, 2002.

Coppinger, Raymond, and Lorna Coppinger. *Dogs: A Startling New Understanding of Canine Origin, Behavior and Evolution.* New York: Scribner, 2001.

Crockford, Susan Janet, ed. *Dogs Through Time: An Archaeological Perspective (the Proceedings of the 1st ICAZ Symposium on the History of the Domestic Dog).* Oxford: BAR International Series, 2000.

Crossan, John Dominic. *Jesus: A Revolutionary Biography.* San Francisco: Harper Collins, 1995.

Cunningham, Dave. "So Why Was Earl the Slug Shunned?" *Newsmagazine* 24.30: 34–35.

Daly, Herman, and John B. Cobb Jr. *For the Common Good: Redirecting the Economy Toward Community, the Environment, and a Sustainable Future.* Boston: Beacon, 1989.

Davies, Oliver, ed. *Celtic Spirituality.* New York: Paulist, 1999.

DeLauretis, Teresa. *Alice Doesn't: Feminism, Semiotics, Cinema.* Bloomington: Indiana UP, 1984.

Derrida, Jacques. "The Animal that Therefore I Am (More to Follow)." ("L'Animal que donc je suis (a suivre).") Trans. David Wills. *Critical Inquiry* 28 (Winter 2002): 369–418.

———. "Sending: On Representation." *Social Research* 49.2 (1982): 295–326.

Descartes, René. *The Philosophical Writings of Descartes.* Trans. John Cottingham, Robert Stoothoff, and Dugald Murdoch. 3 vols. Cambridge: Cambridge UP, 1985.

Di Monte Santa Maria, Ugolino. *The Little Flowers of Saint Francis of Assisi.* Ed. and trans. W. Heywood. New York: Vintage Books, 1998.

Doran, Robert, trans. *The Lives of Simeon Stylites.* Kalamazoo, Mich.: Cistercian, 1992.

Duchet-Suchaux, G., and M. Pastoureau. *The Bible and the Saints: Flammarion Iconographic Guides.* Paris: Flammarion, 1994.

Dunkerley, Roderic. *Beyond the Gospels.* London: Pelican, 1957.

Ehrman, Bart. *After the New Testament: A Reader in Early Christianity.* New York: Oxford UP, 1999.

———. *Lost Christianities: The Battles for Scripture and the Faiths We Never Knew.* New York: Oxford UP, 2003.

Eimerl, Sarel. *The World of Giotto: C. 1267–1337.* Alexandria: Time-Life, 1967.

Elliott, J. K., ed. *The Apocryphal New Testament.* Oxford: Oxford UP, 1993.

Estrada, William. "Los Angeles' Old Plaza and Olvera Street: Imagined and Contested Space." *Western Folklore* 58 (Winter 1999): 107–29.

Ferreiro, Alberto. "Simon Mague, Dogs, and Simon Peter." *The Devil, Heresy and Witchcraft in the Middle Ages: Essays in Honor of Jeffrey B. Russell.* Ed. Alberto Ferreiro. Leiden: Brill, 1998.

Fiorenza, Elisabeth Schussler. *In Memory of Her: A Feminist Theological Reconstruction of Christian Origins.* New York: Crossroad, 1983.

Foucault, Michel. *The Order of Things: An Archaeology of the Human Sciences.* New York: Vintage, 1994.

Fox, Michael W. *Factory Farming.* Washington, D.C.: Humane Society of the United States, 1980.

———. "Agriculture, Livestock and Biotechnology: Values, Profits and Ethics." Waldau and Patton, *Communion of Subjects* 566–67.

Fraser, David. "The New Perception of Animal Agriculture: Legless Cows, Featherless Chickens, and a Need for Genuine Analysis." *Journal of Animal Science* 79 (2001): 634–41.

Frye, Marilyn. "In and Out of Harm's Way." *The Politics of Reality.* Ed. Marilyn Frye. New York: Crossing. 52–83.

Fudge, Erica. *Renaissance Beasts: Of Animals, Humans, and Other Wonderful Creatures.* Urbana: U of Illinois P, 2004.

Geertz, Clifford. *The Interpretation of Cultures.* New York: Basic, 1973.

———. "Deep Play: Notes on the Balinese Cockfight." *Readings in Ritual Studies.* Ed. Ronald L. Grimes. Upper Saddle River: Princeton-Hall, 1996. 217–29.

Germond, Philippe, and Jacques Livet. *An Egyptian Bestiary: Animals in Life and Religion in the Land of the Pharoahs.* London: Thames & Hudson, 2001.

Gibbs, Robert, and Giuliana Fiammetta Tarsi. "Prime rappresentazioni di San Nicola da Tolentiono nella chiesa di San Giacomo a Bologna." *Arte e spiritualit a negli ordini mendicanti; gli Agostiniani e il Cappellone di San Nicola a Tolentino.* Rome, 1992. 195–201.

Gimbutas, Marija. *The Language of the Goddess.* New York: Thames & Hudson, 1989.

———. *The Civilization of the Goddess: The World of Old Europe.* San Francisco: HarperSanFrancisco, 1991.

Gibbs, Robert, Giuliana Fiammetta Tarsi, and Miriam Robbins Dexter. *The Living Goddesses.* Berkeley: U of California Press, 1999.

Glacken, Clarence J. *Traces on the Rhodian Shore: Nature and Culture in Western Thought from Ancient Times to the End of the Eighteenth Century.* Berkeley: U of California P, 1967.

Goodenough, Ursula. *The Sacred Depths of Nature.* New York: Oxford UP, 1998.

Goodfriend, Elaine. "Could *keleb* in Deuteronomy 23:19 Actually Refer to a Canine?" *Pomegranates and Golden Bells; Studies in Biblical, Jewish, and Near Eastern Ritual, Law, and Literature in Honor of Jacob Milgrom.* Winona Lake: Eisenbrauns, 1995. 381–97.

Grant, Robert M. *Early Christians and Animals.* London: Routledge, 1999.

Green, Miranda. *Celtic Goddesses: Warriors, Virgins, and Mothers.* New York: George Braziller, 1996.

Gregory, Timothy. "The Survival of Paganism in Christian Greece: A Critical Essay." *American Journal of Philology* 107.2: 229–42.

Haraway, Donna. *The Companion Species Manifesto: Dogs, People, and Significant Otherness.* Chicago: Prickly Paradigm, 2003.

Harrison, Ruth. *Animal Machines: The New Factory Farming Industry.* London: Stuart, 1964.

Harrod, Howard. *The Animals Came Dancing: Native American Sacred Ecology and Animal Kinship.* Tucson: U of Arizona P, 2000.

Hausman, Gerald, and Loretta Hausman. *The Mythology of Dogs: Canine Legend and Lore Through the Ages.* New York: St. Martin's Griffin, 1997.

Heffernan, Thomas J. *Sacred Biography: Saints and Their Biographers in the Middle Ages.* New York: Oxford UP, 1988.

Hildegard of Bingen. *Scivias.* Trans. Mother Columbia Hart and Jane Bishop. New York: Paulist, 1990.

Houston, Walter. "What Was the Meaning of Classifying Animals as Clean or Unclean?" Linzey and Yamamoto, *Animals on the Agenda* 18–24.

Hennecke, Edgar. *New Testament Apocrypha.* Ed. Wilhelm Schneemelcher. Trans. R. McL. Wilson. Philadelphia: Westminster, 1964.

Huff, Peter A. "Calvin and the Beasts: Animals in John Calvin's Theological Discourse." *Journal of the Evangelical Theological Society* 42.1 (Mar. 1999): 67–75.

Hughes, J. Donald. *Pan's Travail: Environmental Problems of the Ancient Greeks and Romans.* Baltimore: Johns Hopkins UP, 1994.

Ickert, Scott. "Luther and Animals: Subject to Adam's Fall?" Linzey and Yamamoto, *Animals on the Agenda* 90–99.

"Infancy Gospel of Thomas." *Apocryphal New Testament* 68–83.

Jamieson, Anna Brownwell. *Sacred and Legendary Art.* Boston: Houghton, Mifflin, 1900.

Joannides, Paul, and Marianne Sachs. "A 'Last Supper' by the Young Jacopo Bassano and the Sequence of His Early Work." *Burlington Magazine* 133.1063 (Oct. 1991): 695–99.

Jonas, Hans. *The Gnostic Religion: The Message of the Alien God and the Beginnings of Christianity.* Boston: Beacon, 1958.

Jones, Prudence, and Nigel Pennick. *A History of Pagan Europe.* London: Routledge, 1995.

Kieckhefer, Richard, and George D. Bond. *Sainthood: Its Manifestations in World Religions.* Berkleley: U of California P, 1988.

Kienzle, Beverly. "The Bestiary of Heretics: Imaging Medieval Christian Heresy with Insects and Animals." Waldau and Patton, *Communion of Subjects* 103–16.

King, Ynestra. "The Ecology of Feminism and the Feminism of Ecology." *Worldviews, Religion, and the Environment: A Global Anthology.* Ed. Richard Foltz. Belmont, Calif.: Wadsworth, 2003. 457–64.

Klingender, Francis. *Animals in Art and Thought to the End of the Middle Ages.* London: Routledge & Kegan Paul, 1971.

Kolenbrander, Norman. "Mornings at St. Anne's." *Perspectives* Jan. 2000: 5.

Kyle, Donald. *Spectacles of Death in Ancient Rome.* London: Routledge, 1998.

Lawler, Lillian. "A Lion Among Ladies (Theocritus II, 66–68)." *Transactions and Proceedings of the American Philological Association* 78 (1947): 88–98.

Leach, Edmund. "Anthropological Aspects of Language: Animal Categories and Verbal Abuse." *Reader in Comparative Religion: An Anthropological Approach.* Ed. William Lessa and Evon Vogt. New York: Harper and Row, 1958. 206–20.

Lewine, Carol. *The Sistine Chapel Walls and the Roman Liturgy.* University Park: Pennsylvania State UP, 1993.

Lewis, Suzanne. "Sacred Calligraphy: The Chi Rho Page in the Book of Kells." *Traditio: Studies in Ancient and Medieval History, Thought and Religion.* Ed. R. E. Kaske and Charles Lohr. New York: Fordham UP, 1980. 139–59.

Linzey, Andrew. *Animal Gospel.* Louisville, Ky.: Westminster John Knox, 1999.

———. *Animal Theology.* Chicago: U of Illinois P, 1995.

Linzey, Andrew, and Paul Barry Clarke, eds. *Animal Rights: A Historical Anthology.* New York: Columbia UP, 1990.

Linzey, Andrew, and Dan Cohn-Sherbok. *After Noah: Animals and the Liberation of Theology.* London: Mowbray, 1997.

Linzey, Andrew, and Tom Regan, eds. *Animals and Christianity: A Book of Readings.* New York: Crossroad, 1990.

Linzey, Andrew, and Dorothy Yamamoto, eds. *Animals on the Agenda: Questions about Animals for Theology and Ethics.* Urbana: U of Illinois P, 1998.

———. "C. S. Lewis's Theology of Animals." *Anglican Theological Review* 80.1 (Winter 1998): 60–82.

Livingstone, A. "The Isin 'Dog House' Revisited." *Journal of Cuneiform Studies* 40: (1988): 54–60.

MacKinnon, Catharine. "Of Mice and Men: A Feminist Fragment on Animal Rights." *Animal Rights: Current Debates and New Directions.* Ed. Cass R. Sunstein and Martha C. Nussbaum. New York: Oxford UP, 2004.

MacMullen, Ramsay. *Christianity and Paganism in the Fourth to Eighth Centuries.* New Haven: Yale UP, 1997.

MacMullen, Ramsay, and Eugene N. Lane, eds. *Paganism and Christianity: 100–425 C.E.* Minneapolis: Fortress, 1992.

Mancinelli, Fabrizio. *The Sistine Chapel.* Citta del Vaticano: Edizioni Musei Vaticani, 1993.

Marrow, James. "*Circumdederunt me canes multi:* Christ's Tormentors in North European Art of the Late Middle Ages and Early Renaissance." *Art Bulletin* 59.2 (June 1977): 167–81.

Marvin, Garry. "Guest Editor's Introduction: Seeing, Looking, Watching, Observing Non-human Animals." *Society & Animals* 13.1 (2005): 1–12.

Mathews, Thomas. *The Clash of the Gods.* Princeton: Princeton UP, 1993.

McBrien, Richard. *Lives of the Saints.* San Francisco: HarperSanFrancisco, 2001.

McCullough, Florence. *Medieval Latin and French Bestiaries.* Chapel Hill: U of North Carolina P, 1960.

McDaniel, Jay B. *Of God and Pelicans: A Theology of Reverence for Life.* Louisville: Westminster/John Knox, 1989.

———. *Earth, Sky, Gods, and Mortals: A Theology of Ecology for the Twenty-first Century.* Mystic: Twenty-Third Publications, 1990.

McFague, Sallie. *The Body of God: An Ecological Theology.* Minneapolis: Augsburg Fortress, 1993.

McKinley, Phyllis. *Saint-Watching.* New York: Viking, 1969.

McMurrough, Carola. "Blessing of Animals: Roman Rite." *Orate fraters* 14.2 (Dec. 1939): 83–86.

Meeks, Wayne A. *The First Urban Christians: The Social World of the Apostle Paul.* New Haven: Yale UP, 1983.

Meiss, Millard. *The Great Age of Fresco: Discoveries, Recoveries, and Survivals.* New York: Braziller, 1970.

Merchant, Carolyn. *The Death of Nature: Women, Ecology and the Scientific Revolution.* San Francisco: HarperSanFrancisco, 1980.

Metzger, B. M. "St. Paul and the Baptized Lion." *Princeton Seminary Bulletin* 39 (1945): 11–21.

Miles, Margaret. *Carnal Knowing: Female Nakedness and Religious Meaning in the Christian West.* New York: Vintage, 1991.

Milis, Ludo J. R., ed. *The Pagan Middle Ages.* Woodbridge: Boydell, 1998.

Miziolek, Jerzy. "Europa and the Winged Mercury on Two Cassone Panels from the Czartoryski Collection." *Journal of the Warburg and Courtauld Institutes* 56 (1993): 63–74.

Montalembert, Charles Forbes, comte de. *The Monks of the West.* Edinburgh: Blackwood, 1861.

Mulvey, Laura. "Visual Pleasure and Narrative Cinema." *Visual and Other Pleasures.* London: Macmillan, 1989.

Nigosian, S. A. "Zoroastrian Perception of Ascetic Culture." *Journal of Asian and African Studies* 34.1 (Feb. 1999): 4–18.

Oelschlaeger, Max. *The Idea of Wilderness: From Prehistory to the Age of Ecology.* New Haven: Yale UP, 1991.

Olley, John. "Mixed Blessings for Animals: The Contrasts of Genesis 9." *The Earth Story in Genesis.* Ed. Norman Habel and Shirley Wurst. Sheffield, England: Sheffield Academic Press, 2000. 130–39.

Peaceable Kingdom: The Journey Home. Documentary. Prod. Tribe of Heart and Farm Sanctuary, 2004.

Pelikan, Jaroslav. *Luther's Works: Luther the Expositor.* Companion volume. St. Louis: Concordia, 1959.

Pinches, Charles, and Jay B. McDaniel, eds. *Good News for Animals? Christian Approaches to Animal Well-Being.* Maryknoll: Orbis, 1993.

Polzer, Joseph. "Andrea di Bonaiuto's Via Veritatis and Dominican Thought in Late Medieval Italy." *Art Bulletin* 77.2 (1995): 262–89.

Richardson, Cyril, ed. *Early Christian Fathers.* Philadelphia: Westminster, 1953.

Roberts, Alexander, and James Donaldson. *Ante-Nicene Fathers.* 10 vols. New York: Scribner's and Sons, 1926.

Robinson, James M., ed. *The Nag Hammadi Library.* San Francisco: Harper, 1990.

Romanini, Angiola Maria. *Assisi: The Frescoes in the Basilica of St. Francis.* New York: Rizzoli, 1998.

Rosand, David. *Painting in Cinquecento Venice: Titian, Veronese, Tintoretto.* New Haven: Yale UP, 1982.

Ruether, Rosemary Radford, and Rosemary Keller, eds. *In Our Own Voices: Four Centuries of American Women's Religious Writing.* San Francisco: HarperSanFrancisco, 1995.

Ryder, Richard D. *Animal Revolution: Changing Attitudes Towards Speciesism.* New York: Oxford UP, 2000.

Santmire, H. Paul. *The Travail of Nature: The Ambiguous Ecological Promise of Christian Theology.* Philadelphia: Fortress, 1985.

Schimmel, Annemarie. "Cairo Cats." *Saudi Aramco World* 54.3 (May/June 2003): 34–37.

Schmitt, Jean-Claude. *The Holy Greyhound: Guinefort, Healer of Children since the Thirteenth Century.* Trans. Martin Thom. Cambridge: Cambridge UP, 1983.

Scully, Matthew. *Dominion: The Power of Man, the Suffering of Animals, and the Call to Mercy.* New York: St. Martin's, 2002.

Singer, Peter, ed. *In Defence of Animals.* Oxford: Blackwell, 1985.

Smith, Christopher. "Dead Dogs and Rattles; Time, Space and Ritual Sacrifice in Iron Age Latium." *Approaches to the Study of Ritual.* Ed. John Wilkins. London: Accordia Research Centre, 1996. 73–89.

Smith, Jonathan Z. "The Bare Facts of Ritual." In *Readings in Ritual Studies.* Ed. Ronald L. Grimes. Upper Saddle River: Princeton-Hall, 1996. 473–83.

Sluhovsky, Moshe. "The Devil in the Convent." *American Historical Review.* (Dec. 2002): 1379–1411.

Spiegel, Marjorie. *The Dreaded Comparison: Human and Animal Slavery.* New York: Mirror, 1996.

Spranger, J. A. "The Festival of San Zopito and the Ox at Loreto Aprutino." *Journal of the Royal Anthropological Institute of Great Britain and Ireland* 52 (July–Dec. 1922): 306–19.

Stager, Lawrence. "Why Were Hundreds of Dogs Buried at Ashkelon?" *Biblical Archaeology Review* 17.4: 34–53.

Stegemann, Ekkehard, and Wolfgang Stegemann. *The Jesus Movement: A Social History of Its First Century.* Minneapolis: Fortress, 1999.

Steinberg, Leo. "Leonardo's *Last Supper.*" *Art Quarterly* 36 (1973): 297–381.

Szoverffy, Joseph. "The Well of the Holy Women: Some St. Columba Traditions in the West of Ireland." *Journal of American Folklore* 68.268: 111–22.

Tappert, Theodore, ed and trans. *Luther's Works.* Vol. 54. Philadelphia: Fortress, 1957.

Thompson, Leonard. "The Martyrdom of Polycarp: Death in the Roman Games." *Journal of Religion* 82.1: 27–52.

Thurston, Mary Elizabeth. *The Lost History of the Canine Race: Our 15,000-Year Love Affair with Dogs.* Kansas City: Andrews and McMeel, 1996.

Trout, Dennis. "Christianizing the Nolan Countryside: Animal Sacrifice at the Tomb of Saint Felix." *Journal of Early Christian Studies* 3 (Fall 1995): 281–98.

Valcanover, Francesco, and Terisio Pignatti. *Tintoretto.* New York: Abrams, 1985.

Van Engen, John. "The Christian Middle Ages as an Historiographical Problem." *American Historical Review* 91.3: 519–52.

Van de Sandt, Huub. "'Do Not Give What Is Holy to the Dogs' (Did 9:5D and Matt 7:6A): The Eucharistic Food of the Didache in Its Jewish Purity Setting." *Vigiliae Christianae* 56: 223–46.

Vila, Charles, and Peter Savolainen. "Multiple and Ancient Origins of the Domestic Dog." *Science* 276.5319 (June 13, 1997): 1687–90.

Vivian, Tim. "The Peaceable Kingdom: Animals as Parables in the *Virtues of Saint Macarius.*" *Anglican Theological Review* 85.3: 477–91.

Voragine, Jacobus. *The Golden Legend: Readings on the Saints.* Vols. 1 and 2. Trans. William Granger Ryan. Princeton: Princeton UP, 1993.

Waddell, Helen. *Beasts and Saints.* London: Constable, 1934.

Waldau, Paul. *The Specter of Speciesism: Buddhist and Christian Views of Animals.* New York: Oxford UP, 2002.

Waldau, Paul, and Kimberly Patton, eds. *A Communion of Subjects: Animals in Religion, Science, and Ethics.* New York: Columbia UP, 2006.

Walker, Alice. "The Universe Responds." *At Home on the Earth.* Ed. David Landis Barnhill. Berkeley: U of California P, 1999.

Wapnish, Paula, and Brian Hesse. "Pampered Pooches or Plain Pariahs? The Ashkelon Dog Burials." *Biblical Archaeologist* 56.2 (1993): 55–80.

Webb, Stephen. *On God and Dogs: A Christian Theology of Compassion for Animals.* New York: Oxford UP, 1998.

White, Lynn, Jr. "The Historical Roots of our Ecological Crisis." *Science.* 155 (Mar. 1967): 1203–7.

Wiedeman, Thomas. *Emperors and Gladiators.* London: Routledge, 1992.

Williams, Charles, ed. *The Letters of Evelyn Underhill.* London: Longmans, Green, 1943.

Williams, Michael Allen. *Rethinking "Gnosticism": An Argument for Dismantline a Dubious Category.* Princeton: Princeton UP, 1996.

Wintz, Jack. "The Beauty of the Beasts." *U.S. Catholic* 69.10 (October 2004): 49.

Wood, Jeryldene M. *Women, Art, and Spirituality: The Poor Clares of Early Modern Italy.* Cambridge: Cambridge UP, 1996.

Worthen, Thomas. "Tintoretto's Paintings for the Banco del Sacramento in S. Margherita." *Art Bulletin* 78.4 (Dec. 1996): 707–32.

Yamamoto, Dorothy. "Aquinas and Animals: Patrolling the Boundary?" Linzey and Yamamoto, *Animals on the Agenda* 80–99.

Index

LAURA HOBGOOD-OSTER is Elizabeth Root Paden Professor of Religion at Southwestern University. She is author of *She Glanceth from Earth to Heaven* and editor of several volumes, including *The Sabbath Journal of Judith Lomax, Crossroads Choices: Biblical Wisdom Literature into the Twenty-first Century*, and *The Encyclopedia of Religion and Nature.*

The University of Illinois Press
is a founding member of the
Association of American University Presses.

Composed in 10.5/13 Adobe Minion Pro
by Jim Proefrock
at the University of Illinois Press
Manufactured by Thomson-Shore, Inc.

University of Illinois Press
1325 South Oak Street
Champaign, IL 61820-6903
www.press.uillinois.edu